THIS BOOK BELONGS TO

The Library of

....

....

©COPYRIGHT2023

ALL RIGHTS RESERVED

The content contained within this book may not be reproduced, duplicated, or transmitted without direct written permission from the author or the publisher. Under no circumstances will any blame or legal responsibility be held against the publisher, or author, for any damages, reparation, or monetary loss due to the information contained within this book. Either directly or indirectly.

Legal Notice:

This book is copyright protected. This book is only for personal use. You cannot amend, distribute, sell, use, quote, or paraphrase any part, or the content within this book, without the consent of the author or publisher.

Disclaimer Notice:

Please note the information contained within this document is for educational and entertainment purposes only. All effort has been executed to present accurate, up-to-date, and reliable, complete information. No warranties of any kind are declared or implied. Readers acknowledge that the author is not engaging in the rendering of legal, financial, medical, or professional advice. The content within this book has been derived from various sources. Please consult a licensed professional before attempting any techniques outlined in this book. By reading this document, the reader agrees that under no circumstances is the author responsible for any losses, direct or indirect, which are incurred as a result of the use of the information contained within this document, including, but not limited to — errors, omissions, or inaccuracies

I can't tell you how grateful I am that you decided to read my book. My most heartfelt thanks that you took time out of your life to choose my work and I hope you find benefit within these pages.

There are so many books available today that offer similar content so that makes it even more humbling that you decided to buying mine.

Tell me what you thought! I am eager to hear your opinion and ideas on what you read as are others who are looking for a good book to buy. Leave a review on Amazon.com so others can benefit from your wisdom!

With much thanks.

Table of Contents

Introduction to Crochet	26
Supplies Needed	28
Basic Stitch Techniques	32
Using a Pattern	52
Patterns	55
Woven Together Afghan	55
Carry-All Tote Bag	75
Soap Sack	118
Cozy Cowl	130
Conclusion	149
Troubleshooting	150

SUMMARY

The timeless art of crochet is a craft that has been passed down through generations, captivating individuals with its intricate designs and endless possibilities. Crochet involves using a hook and yarn to create various stitches and patterns, resulting in beautiful and functional pieces.

One of the most appealing aspects of crochet is its versatility. From delicate doilies and lacy shawls to cozy blankets and warm sweaters, crochet can be used to create a wide range of items. Whether you are looking to adorn your home with handmade decorations or create personalized gifts for loved ones, crochet offers a multitude of options.

The process of crochet is both relaxing and rewarding. As you work with your hands, the rhythmic motions of the hook and yarn can have a calming effect, allowing you to unwind and focus on the present moment. The repetitive nature of crochet also provides a sense of accomplishment as you see your project gradually take shape.

Crochet is a craft that encourages creativity and self-expression. With countless stitch patterns and color combinations to choose from, you can truly make each project your own. Whether you prefer bold and vibrant hues or soft and subtle tones, crochet allows you to experiment and create unique pieces that reflect your personal style.

Furthermore, crochet is a craft that can be enjoyed by individuals of all ages and skill levels. Whether you are a beginner just starting out or an experienced crocheter looking to expand your skills, there are resources available to help you learn and grow. From online tutorials and instructional books to local crochet groups and workshops, the crochet community is welcoming and supportive.

In addition to its artistic and therapeutic benefits, crochet also has practical advantages. Handmade crochet items are often cherished for their durability and quality. Unlike mass-produced items, crochet pieces are made with care and attention to detail, ensuring that they will stand the test of time. Additionally, crochet allows for customization, allowing you to create items that fit perfectly and meet your specific needs.

In conclusion, the timeless art of crochet is a craft that offers endless possibilities for creativity, relaxation, and self-expression. Whether you are drawn to its versatility, therapeutic qualities, or practical advantages, crochet is a rewarding and fulfilling hobby that can be enjoyed by individuals of all ages and skill levels. So grab your hook and yarn, and let your imagination soar as you embark on your crochet journey.

This response was truncated by the cut-off limit (max tokens). Open the sidebar, Increase the parameter in the settings and then regenerate.

Choosing the right yarn and hooks is an essential step in any crochet project. The type of yarn and hook you select can greatly impact the final outcome of your project, including its appearance, texture, and overall durability.

When it comes to choosing the right yarn, there are several factors to consider. First and foremost, you need to think about the fiber content of the yarn. Different fibers have different properties, such as warmth, softness, and drape. For example, if you're making a cozy winter scarf, you might opt for a wool or alpaca yarn for its warmth and softness. On the other hand, if you're making a lightweight summer top, you might choose a cotton or bamboo yarn for its breathability.

Another important consideration is the weight or thickness of the yarn. Yarns come in various weights, ranging from lace weight (the thinnest) to super bulky (the thickest). The weight of the yarn will determine the size of the stitches and the overall look of your project. Thicker yarns will create larger, more substantial stitches, while thinner yarns will result in finer, more delicate stitches. It's important to match the weight of the yarn to the pattern you're using to ensure the desired outcome.

Additionally, you should also take into account the color and texture of the yarn. The color can greatly impact the visual appeal of your project, so choose a color that complements your design or matches your personal style. The texture of the yarn can also add interest and dimension to your project. Some yarns have a smooth, even texture, while others may have a more textured or boucle effect. Consider the desired look and feel of your project when selecting the yarn texture.

Once you've chosen the right yarn, it's time to select the appropriate hook size. The hook size will determine the size of the stitches and the overall tension of your project. Most yarn labels will recommend a hook size range for that particular yarn. It's important to follow these recommendations to achieve the desired gauge and ensure that your project turns out the right size. Using a hook that is too small can result in tight, stiff stitches, while using a hook that is too large can create loose, floppy stitches.

In conclusion, choosing the right yarn and hooks is crucial for the success of your crochet project. Consider factors such as fiber content, weight, color, and texture when selecting your yarn.

This response was truncated by the cut-off limit (max tokens). Open the sidebar, Increase the parameter in the settings and then regenerate.

When it comes to joining yarn and changing colors in your knitting or crochet project, there are a few techniques you can use to ensure a smooth transition and secure connection.

Firstly, when joining a new ball of yarn, it's important to choose a suitable method that will prevent any loose ends or knots from unraveling. One common technique is the "Russian join," which involves threading the tail of the new yarn through the plies of the old yarn, creating a secure and seamless join. Another option is the "spit splice," which works well with certain types of yarn, such as wool, by moistening the ends and rubbing them together to create a felted connection.

If you prefer a more traditional method, you can simply tie a knot to join the new yarn to the old one. However, it's crucial to ensure that the knot is tight enough to prevent it from coming undone during use, but not too tight that it distorts the fabric.

Additionally, you may want to leave a tail of at least a few inches to weave in later, ensuring a neat and tidy finish.

When it comes to changing colors in your project, there are a few techniques you can employ to achieve a clean and professional look. One popular method is the "intarsia" technique, which involves using separate balls of yarn for each color section. This technique is commonly used in colorwork patterns, such as Fair Isle or stranded knitting, and allows for precise color placement and minimal yarn floats on the wrong side of the fabric.

Another technique for changing colors is the "slip stitch" method, which is often used in crochet projects. With this method, you simply slip stitch into the next stitch with the new color, effectively changing colors without any visible transition lines. This technique works well for creating stripes or color blocks in your crochet work.

In both knitting and crochet, it's important to carry the unused yarn along the back of your work when changing colors. This helps to prevent long floats or loose strands from snagging or getting caught. You can achieve this by twisting the two yarns together at the beginning of each row or round, ensuring a secure connection and minimizing any gaps or holes in your fabric.

Overall, joining yarn and changing colors in your knitting or crochet project requires careful attention to detail and technique. By choosing the appropriate method for your project and taking the time to secure your connections, you can achieve a polished and professional finish that will enhance the overall look of your work.

Maintaining consistent tension refers to the act of keeping a steady and balanced level of pressure or force applied to an object or situation. This concept is applicable in various contexts, such as physical activities, interpersonal relationships, and even in the functioning of mechanical systems.

In physical activities, maintaining consistent tension is crucial for achieving optimal performance and preventing injuries. For example, in weightlifting, maintaining consistent tension in the muscles throughout the movement ensures proper form and maximizes the effectiveness of the exercise. Similarly, in activities like yoga or Pilates, maintaining consistent tension in the core muscles helps stabilize the body and maintain balance during challenging poses.

In interpersonal relationships, maintaining consistent tension is essential for healthy communication and conflict resolution. It involves finding a balance between expressing one's needs and emotions while also being mindful of the other person's feelings and boundaries. By maintaining consistent tension in communication, individuals can avoid extremes of aggression or passivity, fostering a more harmonious and productive exchange of ideas and emotions.

In mechanical systems, maintaining consistent tension is crucial for the smooth operation and longevity of various components. For instance, in a conveyor belt system, maintaining consistent tension ensures that the belt remains properly aligned and prevents slippage or damage. Similarly, in a guitar or piano, maintaining consistent tension in the strings is essential for producing accurate and pleasing sounds.

Overall, maintaining consistent tension is a fundamental principle that applies to a wide range of activities and situations. It promotes efficiency, effectiveness, and harmony, whether it be in physical activities, interpersonal relationships, or mechanical systems. By understanding and practicing this concept, individuals can enhance their performance, communication skills, and the functionality of various systems.

This response was truncated by the cut-off limit (max tokens). Open the sidebar, Increase the parameter in the settings and then regenerate.

For the input of a simple scarf or cowl, the output can be a versatile and stylish accessory that adds warmth and flair to any outfit. A scarf is typically a long and narrow piece of fabric that can be wrapped around the neck in various ways, while a cowl is a circular or tubular garment that can be worn around the neck like a turtleneck or pulled up over the head as a hood.

When it comes to choosing the fabric for a simple scarf or cowl, there are numerous options available. One can opt for a cozy and warm material like wool or cashmere for those chilly winter days, or choose a lighter fabric such as cotton or silk for a more breathable and lightweight accessory. The choice of fabric can greatly impact the overall look and feel of the scarf or cowl, allowing for customization based on personal preferences and the intended use.

In terms of design, a simple scarf or cowl can be as basic or intricate as desired. For those who prefer a minimalist style, a plain and solid-colored scarf or cowl can be the perfect choice. On the other hand, those who enjoy a more elaborate look can opt for a patterned or textured fabric, or even experiment with different knitting or crochet techniques to create unique and eye-catching designs.

The versatility of a simple scarf or cowl is truly remarkable. It can be worn in a variety of ways, allowing for endless styling possibilities. A scarf can be draped loosely around the neck for a casual and effortless look, or wrapped tightly for added warmth and a more polished appearance. A cowl can be worn as a statement piece, adding a touch of elegance and sophistication to any ensemble. It can also be pulled up over the head to protect against the elements, making it a practical choice for those colder days.

Furthermore, a simple scarf or cowl can be a great accessory for both men and women, making it a versatile option for anyone looking to enhance their wardrobe. It can be paired with a coat or jacket during the colder months, or worn with a simple t-shirt or blouse to add a pop of color and style to an everyday outfit. The possibilities are truly endless when it comes to incorporating a simple scarf or cowl into one's wardrobe.

In conclusion, a simple scarf or cowl can be a fantastic addition to any wardrobe. With a wide range of fabric choices, design options, and styling possibilities, it is a versatile accessory that can be customized to suit individual preferences and needs.

This response was truncated by the cut-off limit (max tokens). Open the sidebar, Increase the parameter in the settings and then regenerate.

A lace shawl or wrap is a versatile and elegant accessory that adds a touch of sophistication to any outfit. Made from delicate lace fabric, it is typically lightweight and sheer, making it perfect for layering over dresses, blouses, or even casual tops. The intricate lace patterns and designs give it a feminine and romantic appeal, making it a popular choice for special occasions such as weddings, parties, or formal events.

One of the key features of a lace shawl or wrap is its versatility. It can be worn in various ways, allowing you to experiment with different styles and looks. You can drape it over your shoulders for a classic and timeless look, or wrap it around your neck as a scarf for added warmth and style. It can also be worn as a sarong or a beach cover-up, making it a must-have accessory for vacations or trips to the beach.

The delicate and intricate lace patterns of a shawl or wrap add a touch of elegance and femininity to any outfit. Whether it's a simple black dress or a casual jeans and t-shirt ensemble, adding a lace shawl instantly elevates the overall look. The sheer fabric allows for a subtle peek-a-boo effect, adding a hint of allure and sophistication.

In terms of materials, lace shawls or wraps are typically made from high-quality fabrics such as cotton, silk, or synthetic blends. These materials ensure durability and longevity, allowing you to enjoy your lace shawl for years to come. Additionally, the lightweight nature of the fabric makes it easy to fold and pack, making it a convenient accessory to carry with you wherever you go.

When it comes to styling, a lace shawl or wrap can be paired with a wide range of outfits. For a formal event, you can pair it with a cocktail dress or an evening gown to add a touch of glamour. For a more casual look, you can wear it with jeans, a blouse, and heels for a chic and sophisticated ensemble. The versatility of a lace shawl or wrap allows you to effortlessly transition from day to night, making it a valuable addition to your wardrobe.

In conclusion, a lace shawl or wrap is a timeless and elegant accessory that adds a touch of femininity and sophistication to any outfit. Its delicate lace patterns, lightweight fabric, and versatility make it a must-have accessory for any fashion-conscious individual. Whether you're attending a formal event or simply want to elevate your everyday look.

A. An intricate doily or table runner is a delicate and ornate piece of textile art that is typically used to adorn tables or other surfaces. It is meticulously crafted with intricate patterns and designs, often featuring delicate lacework or embroidery. The level of detail and complexity in these pieces is truly remarkable, showcasing the skill and craftsmanship of the maker.

The doily or table runner is usually made from fine materials such as cotton, linen, or silk, which adds to its elegance and sophistication. The choice of material can greatly impact the overall appearance and feel of the piece. For instance, a doily made from silk will have a luxurious and smooth texture, while one made from cotton may have a more rustic and casual feel.

The patterns and designs found on these doilies and table runners can vary greatly, ranging from simple geometric shapes to intricate floral motifs. Some designs may be symmetrical, while others may have a more asymmetrical or abstract composition. The patterns are often created using techniques such as crochet, tatting, or bobbin lace, requiring great precision and attention to detail.

These intricate doilies and table runners are not only decorative but also serve a practical purpose. They can protect the surface they are placed on from scratches or stains, making them ideal for use on delicate or valuable furniture. Additionally, they can add a touch of elegance and sophistication to any room or table setting, instantly elevating the overall aesthetic.

Due to their intricate nature, these doilies and table runners are often considered heirloom pieces, passed down through generations as cherished family treasures. They can hold sentimental value and serve as a reminder of the skill and artistry of the maker. Many people also choose to display these pieces as works of art, framing them or placing them under glass to preserve their beauty.

In conclusion, an intricate doily or table runner is a stunning piece of textile art that showcases the skill and craftsmanship of the maker. With their delicate patterns and designs, fine materials, and practical functionality, these pieces add a touch of elegance and sophistication to any space. Whether used as a decorative accent or cherished as a family heirloom, these intricate doilies and table runners are truly a testament to the beauty of handmade craftsmanship.

A. Pillow covers and cushion designs are essential elements in home decor that can instantly transform the look and feel of any space. These decorative accessories not only provide comfort and support but also add a touch of style and personality to your living room, bedroom, or any other area where you use them.

When it comes to pillow covers, there is a wide range of options available to suit different tastes and preferences. From solid colors to intricate patterns, you can find pillow covers in various materials such as cotton, silk, velvet, or even leather. The choice of fabric depends on the overall theme and ambiance you want to create in your room. For a cozy and warm atmosphere, you might opt for soft and plush materials like velvet or faux fur. On the other hand, if you prefer a more contemporary and sleek look, cotton or linen pillow covers can be a great choice.

In addition to the fabric, the design and pattern of the pillow covers also play a significant role in enhancing the aesthetic appeal of your space. You can choose from a wide array of options, including geometric prints, floral motifs, abstract designs, or even personalized patterns. The design you select should complement the existing color scheme and furniture in your room. For instance, if you have a minimalist decor with neutral tones, you might want to opt for pillow covers with bold and vibrant patterns to create a focal point.

Cushion designs, on the other hand, refer to the shape and structure of the cushions themselves. While square and rectangular cushions are the most common shapes, you can also find round, oval, or even novelty-shaped cushions to add a unique touch to your decor. The size of the cushions should be chosen based on the furniture they will be placed on and the level of comfort you desire.

Larger cushions are perfect for lounging and relaxation, while smaller ones are ideal for adding a decorative touch to chairs or sofas.

When selecting pillow covers and cushion designs, it is important to consider the overall theme and style of your home. Whether you prefer a traditional, modern, or eclectic look, there are countless options available to suit your taste. Additionally, don't be afraid to mix and match different patterns, textures, and colors to create a visually appealing and personalized space. Remember, pillow covers and cushion designs are not only functional but also serve as decorative accents that can elevate the overall ambiance of your home.

One possible output for fixing tension issues is to first identify the source of the tension. This could be due to a variety of factors such as stress, poor communication, conflicting goals, or unresolved conflicts. Once the source is identified, it is important to address it directly and openly.

One approach to fixing tension issues is to promote open and honest communication within the team or organization. This can be achieved by creating a safe and non-judgmental environment where team members feel comfortable expressing their concerns and opinions. Regular team meetings or one-on-one discussions can be scheduled to provide a platform for open dialogue.

Another strategy for fixing tension issues is to encourage collaboration and teamwork. By fostering a sense of unity and shared goals, team members are more likely to work together towards resolving conflicts and reducing tension. This can be achieved through team-building activities, promoting a positive work culture, and providing opportunities for team members to collaborate on projects.

In some cases, tension issues may require mediation or conflict resolution techniques. This could involve bringing in a neutral third party to facilitate discussions and help find a resolution that satisfies all parties involved. Mediation can be particularly useful when tensions are high and communication has broken down.

Additionally, it is important to address any underlying causes of tension. This could involve providing additional training or resources to team members who may be struggling with their roles or responsibilities. It may also be necessary to reevaluate goals and expectations to ensure they are realistic and achievable.

Overall, fixing tension issues requires a proactive and collaborative approach. By promoting open communication, fostering teamwork, and addressing underlying causes, it is possible to reduce tension and create a more harmonious work environment.

This response was truncated by the cut-off limit (max tokens). Open the sidebar, Increase the parameter in the settings and then regenerate.

A. A showcase of stunning crochet projects is a visually captivating display of intricate and beautifully crafted pieces that have been meticulously created using the art of crochet. This collection of projects serves as a testament to the skill, creativity, and dedication of the individuals who have poured their time and effort into mastering this age-old craft.

Each crochet project featured in this showcase is a work of art in its own right, showcasing the versatility and endless possibilities that can be achieved with a simple hook and a ball of yarn. From delicate lace doilies to cozy blankets, from intricate shawls to adorable amigurumi toys, this collection encompasses a wide range of crochet techniques and styles.

The attention to detail in these projects is truly awe-inspiring. Every stitch, loop, and pattern has been carefully chosen and executed to create a visually stunning and cohesive piece. The color choices are vibrant and harmonious, adding depth and dimension to the finished projects. The texture created through various crochet stitches adds an extra layer of interest and tactile appeal.

What sets this showcase apart is not only the beauty of the finished projects but also the stories behind them. Each piece has its own unique journey, from the initial spark of inspiration to the hours spent selecting the perfect yarn, to the countless moments of concentration and patience required to bring the project to life. The passion and love poured into each stitch are palpable, making these crochet projects not just objects, but cherished heirlooms and treasured gifts.

This showcase serves as a source of inspiration for both seasoned crochet enthusiasts and those new to the craft. It offers a glimpse into the endless possibilities that can be achieved through crochet, encouraging individuals to explore their own creativity and push the boundaries of what they thought was possible. Whether you are looking to embark on your first crochet project or seeking new ideas to challenge your skills, this showcase is sure to ignite your imagination and leave you in awe of the incredible talent and artistry that exists within the world of crochet.

In conclusion, a showcase of stunning crochet projects is a celebration of the artistry, skill, and creativity that goes into creating these beautiful pieces. It is a testament to the dedication and passion of the individuals who have mastered the craft of crochet and a source of inspiration for those looking to embark on their own crochet journey. From delicate lace doilies to cozy blankets, this showcase offers a glimpse into the limitless possibilities that can be achieved through crochet.

This response was truncated by the cut-off limit (max tokens). Open the sidebar, Increase the parameter in the settings and then regenerate.

Reflecting on my crochet journey, I can't help but feel a sense of pride and accomplishment. It all started several years ago when I stumbled upon a crochet tutorial online. Intrigued by the intricate patterns and beautiful creations, I decided to give it a try. Little did I know that this simple decision would lead me on a transformative journey of creativity and self-discovery.

In the beginning, I struggled to grasp the basic stitches and techniques. The yarn slipped through my fingers, and my hands felt clumsy and uncoordinated. However, with each failed attempt, I became more determined to master this craft. I spent countless hours practicing, watching tutorials, and seeking advice from experienced crocheters. Slowly but surely, my skills began to improve.

As I gained confidence in my abilities, I started experimenting with different patterns and designs. From simple scarves and hats to intricate blankets and amigurumi, I challenged myself to push the boundaries of what I thought was possible. Each project became a canvas for my creativity, allowing me to express myself in ways I never thought possible.

Crocheting also became a form of therapy for me. In the midst of life's chaos and stress, I found solace in the rhythmic motion of my hook and yarn. The repetitive nature of crochet provided a sense of calm and mindfulness, allowing me to escape from the outside world and focus solely on the present moment. It became a form of meditation, a way to quiet my mind and find inner peace.

But perhaps the most rewarding aspect of my crochet journey has been the connections I've made along the way. I've joined online communities and local crochet groups, where I've met fellow enthusiasts who share the same passion for this craft. We've exchanged tips, patterns, and stories, forming a tight-knit community that supports and inspires one another. Through crochet, I've found a sense of belonging and camaraderie that I never expected.

Looking back on how far I've come, I am filled with a sense of gratitude. Crochet has not only provided me with a creative outlet but has also taught me valuable life lessons. It has taught me patience, perseverance, and the importance of embracing imperfections. It has shown me that with dedication and practice, I can turn a simple strand of yarn into something beautiful and meaningful.

As I continue on my crochet journey, I am excited to see where it will take me next. There are endless possibilities and new techniques to explore.

This response was truncated by the cut-off limit (max tokens). Open the sidebar, Increase the parameter in the settings and then regenerate.

Crochet, as a form of creative expression, holds immense potential for continuous exploration and innovation. It is a craft that allows individuals to transform simple strands of yarn into intricate and beautiful creations. To encourage and foster continuous creativity in crochet, it is important to provide a supportive environment that values experimentation, learning, and growth.

One way to promote continuous creativity in crochet is by encouraging individuals to step out of their comfort zones and try new techniques or patterns. By challenging themselves to learn unfamiliar stitches or tackle complex projects, crocheters can expand their skill set and discover new possibilities. This can be achieved through workshops, online tutorials, or joining crochet communities where experienced crafters can share their knowledge and inspire others to push their boundaries.

Another aspect of encouraging continuous creativity in crochet is by providing a platform for crocheters to showcase their work and receive feedback. This can be done through local craft fairs, online forums, or social media platforms dedicated to crochet. By receiving constructive criticism and positive reinforcement, crocheters can gain valuable insights and motivation to further refine their skills and explore new ideas.

Furthermore, it is important to emphasize the importance of self-expression in crochet. Encouraging individuals to infuse their own personal style and creativity into their projects can lead to unique and innovative designs. By celebrating individuality and encouraging crocheters to trust their instincts, we can inspire a culture of continuous exploration and creativity in the crochet community.

Additionally, providing resources and inspiration for crocheters is crucial in fostering continuous creativity. This can include access to a wide range of crochet patterns, books, magazines, and online platforms that showcase different styles and techniques. By exposing crocheters to diverse sources of inspiration, they can expand their creative horizons and develop their own unique voice in the craft.

Lastly, it is important to create a supportive and inclusive community for crocheters to connect and collaborate with one another. By organizing crochet meetups, workshops, or online communities, individuals can share their experiences, exchange ideas, and collaborate on projects. This sense of community not only provides a space for continuous learning and growth but also serves as a source of encouragement and motivation for crocheters to keep exploring and pushing their creative boundaries.

In conclusion, encouraging continuous creativity and exploration in crochet requires creating a supportive environment that values experimentation, learning, and growth. By providing opportunities for individuals to try new techniques, receive feedback, express their personal style.

How to Crochet
A Beginner's Guide to Crocheting with step-by-step patters and projects

Text Copyright © Lightbulb Publishing

All rights reserved. No part of this guide may be reproduced in any form without permission in writing from the publisher except in the case of brief quotations embodied in critical articles or reviews.

Legal & Disclaimer

The information contained in this book and its contents is not designed to replace or take the place of any form of medical or professional advice; and is not meant to replace the need for independent medical, financial, legal or other professional advice or services, as may be required. The content and information in this book has been provided for educational and entertainment purposes only.

The content and information contained in this book has been compiled from sources deemed reliable, and it is accurate to the best of the Author's knowledge, information, and belief. However, the Author cannot guarantee its accuracy and validity and cannot be held liable for any errors and/or omissions. Further, changes are periodically made to this book as and when needed. Where appropriate and/or necessary, you must consult a professional (including but not limited to your doctor, attorney, financial advisor or such other professional advisor) before using any of the suggested remedies, techniques, or information in this book.

Upon using the contents and information contained in this book, you agree to hold harmless the Author from and against any damages, costs, and expenses, including any legal fees potentially resulting from the application of any of the information provided by this book. This disclaimer applies to any loss, damages or injury caused by the use and application, whether directly or indirectly, of any advice or information presented, whether for breach of contract, tort, negligence, personal injury, criminal intent, or under any other cause of action.

You agree to accept all risks of using the information presented in this book.

You agree that by continuing to read this book, where appropriate and/or necessary, you shall consult a professional (including but not limited to your doctor, attorney, or financial advisor or such other advisor as needed) before using any of the suggested remedies, techniques, or information in this book.

Introduction to Crochet

Crochet: a French word meaning "small hook."

Crocheting is a noble art that was once common. Grandmothers would teach their children and grandchildren how to crochet. Wives and mothers would be proud of the things they would create for their homes.

A lot has changed since the invention of crochet when people crocheted out of necessity. Back then, crocheting was primarily seen as a women's craft. In today's world, we most often crochet for the sheer fun of it and now the craft is enjoyed by all people who give it a try, regardless of gender.

Crocheting is a fun and relaxing craft that is enjoyed the world over. Nearly every town that you visit will have at least one craft store that supplies beautiful yarns, threads, and all other necessary materials for the needle arts.

To summarize it as concisely as possible, crocheting is the art of taking yarn and a hook and forming a knotted fabric from it. Using a few basic stitches, you can create a myriad of items that are both lovely and useful. Every single crocheted item is made of variations of the five basic stitches: *chain, single crochet, half double crochet, double crochet, and slip stitch*. As you become more skilled in the craft, you will learn new ways of using and combining these stitches, to create a variety of products. With more advanced techniques, your fabrics will be stunningly sophisticated, yet amazingly simple.

Crocheting has been called many things throughout history: netting, knotting, filet, needle-coiling, or looped needle-knotting. The materials used were rough and crude, including hair, spun wool, hemp, grass, and flax. The most common hooks were made from bone or wood, and at times the rich and wealthy would boast of ivory hooks. Nowadays, we have hooks fashioned out of metal, bamboo, stainless steel, aluminum, plastic, wood, and silicone. They come in various shapes and sizes, with different grips and tips. The crochet hooks of today are more comfortable to hold and use for hours than the wooden or bone hooks of yesteryear. There are hooks specialized for those with large hands, small hands, arthritic hands, those with carpal tunnel syndrome — the list is endless. Today's yarns are made of cotton, bamboo, silk, chenille, and linen.

Crocheting is thought to have been invented in the early 1700s by the Turks, who used a hook and a piece of open-weave background fabric to embroider beautiful designs in a method similar to modern crochet. It caught on quickly and spread to the rest of the world from there. In the 1800s, crochet became popular in England, where the thread and hook were used without the background fabric.

In 1845, the Irish developed a new and more refined type of crocheting. Irish Crochet is a delicate and intricate method of crocheting embellishments that the world sought after. Ultimately, this clever new form of crochet helped the Irish stay alive during the potato famine, as they were able to sell the coveted product. This type of crochet involved a thin, slender hook and a very fine thread to produce an exquisitely finished piece.

In the early 1900s, crocheting as we know it came into fashion. Crocheted products such as lace, shawls, and curtains became very popular. Women would fashion hats, scarves, gloves, and socks during the wars to send to their soldier boys to keep them warm and remind them of home.

Slowly but surely, crocheting began to drop out of fashion and was kept alive only by the faithful few. It is only now, in 2020, that crocheting is has broken back into the fashion scene both as a fashion statement and as a hobby. There are so many crocheted accessories that you can purchase, but why not make them yourself? When we create something ourselves, we get to design it exactly the way we want, in the colors we like, to the specifications that we desire.

Crocheting is a beautiful craft. Through crocheting, you can make unique handmade items that friends and family will cherish forever. So, let's give it a try and learn how to create some beautiful things!

Supplies Needed

I don't have a problem with yarn. I have a problem without it!

There are very few supplies required for crocheting. In fact, there are only two: a crochet hook and yarn. Such a simple list, and yet there are so many options available to the beginner. Not to mention all the other lovely accessories that will make a crocheter's life easier. So, which of these many options is the best for starting your needlecraft collection? Which items do you *really* need to start producing lovely projects, and which can you do without purchasing right away?

Hooks

Crochet hooks are made from a wide variety of different materials: wood, bamboo, aluminum, glass, and plastic, to name a few. Specialty hooks can be made with mixed materials for a certain aesthetic, such as clay and aluminum or wood and metal. Specialty hooks tend to be more expensive and harder to learn on, although if you enjoy crocheting, they are a nice addition to your collection.

You will notice that there are several numbers and letters on each hook. The hook size is based on the diameter of the hook and is measured in millimeters (mm). This size is noted in two distinct ways on the hook: the letters and numbers are the American sizes, whereas the millimeters are the European sizes. They are written with both notations because some of the patterns you may run across will have the European notation for the hook size, and you can quickly locate the one you are to use. The sizes are noted in a logical progression: lower number and letter combinations for smaller hooks and higher number and letter combinations for larger hooks.

Typically, crochet hooks smaller than 2mm, or a "D," are made of steel and are called "thread hooks." These are the hooks that are used with crochet thread to make doilies, lace, and other intricate projects. These types of projects are difficult and time-consuming, but worth the effort for intermediate and advanced crocheters!

I would definitely recommend starting with aluminum hooks because they are easier to use than bamboo or wood and allow the yarn to glide smoothly over the hook without snagging. Aluminum hooks are also easier to insert into stitches without splitting your yarn. While they might not as pretty as the others, they certainly are functional. It is for this reason that they are so popular! By contrast, glass and plastic hooks tend to be too slippery and can be frustrating when you are attempting to learn to crochet.

As a beginner purchasing crochet hooks for the first time, you can either buy a whole set of hooks, or just the sizes you need for a specific project. The decision is entirely up to you and based on how much money you want to invest at this stage. When you become a more advanced crocheter, you can purchase one-of-a-kind, beautiful hooks that will last you a lifetime!

Yarn

There are so many options to choose from with yarn! There are millions of colors and millions more possible combinations of colors, a thousand different blends and fibers, and several different weights of yarn from which you can choose. As an avid crocheter, I have bags and bags of yarn shoved into any nook and cranny in my home. Sometimes I buy a specific yarn for a particular project. Other times I run into sales, reasonable prices, and unusual colors that I simply must add to my stash.

Yarn comes in different thicknesses and sizes, known as weights. These weights will be noted on the yarn label. There are eight main weights of yarn to get familiar with:

- #0 / Lace. This type of yarn is also called *lace weight, light weight, and light fingering.* An example of this weight would be something like a thin crochet thread used for making lace and doilies.
- #1 / Super fine. This is also called *fingering,* and this type of yarn is used for making socks, gloves, and lightweight clothing items.

- #2 / Fine. Also called *baby* or *sport*. This type of yarn is ideal for baby garments and lightweight sweaters.
- #3 / Light. This yarn is often used for creating sweaters, scarves, and slippers. Also referred to as *DK weight.*
- #4 / Medium. Also called *worsted* or *Aran*, this yarn is used for afghans, sweaters, scarves, blanket, hats, or gloves. This is a very versatile yarn, and there are so many fun yarn combinations to be found in this weight!
- #5 / Bulky. These thicker yarns are all the rage right now. Though traditionally, these heavier yarns were used to create heavy duty items like rugs, they are becoming more popular for chunky sweaters, heavy blankets, jumbo scarves, and warm jackets. And no wonder — working up projects using the thicker yarn is a breeze! This #5 yarn is also called *Chunky,* or *Craft.*
- #6 / Super Bulky. This is another popular yarn for sweaters and scarves, as chunky items are all in style. Also called *Super Chunky* or *Roving,* this yarn works up quickly.
- #7 / Jumbo. Also called *Roving,* the yarns in the category will be unspun specialty yarns that require special care. They are becoming more popular, and modern crochet patterns will utilize these types of yarn for blankets or afghans.

It is essential to know both the weight and the category of the yarn, as many patterns will simply call for "240 yards of DK weight yarn," and you must figure out which yarn in the aisle is actually DK weight.

When you go out yarn shopping, it's a good idea to have a list of what type of yarn you want to purchase, or else you'll quickly end up like me with more yarn than you could use in a lifetime. That super bulky size 6 yarn may be a lovely color, but if you are looking for yarn suitable for a pair of slippers, you won't want to use that one!

The projects in this book utilize cotton yarn, merino wool, and DK weight yarn — all easy to find and fun to use.

Stitch Markers

Stitch markers are an item that attaches to your work, helping you to keep track of a particular spot in the pattern. This comes especially in handy when you're working in rounds. You can go out and buy some nice stitch markers if you so desire. But I've found that bobby pins, safety pins, little tiny hair elastics, and paper clips will work just as nicely!

Scissors

Enough said! You need something to cut the yarn with, and sharp scissors are a lifesaver! Sharp scissors will keep the ends of the yarn from fraying, causing you less frustration. Tip: make sure you only use your scissors for cutting yarn. Paper and plastic will dull them like nobody's business.

Tape Measure

Another must for your work-bag. You need a good tape measure for measuring the gauge of a project, knowing how many inches you've worked, and just measuring in particular.

Basic Stitch Techniques

Crocheting keeps me from unraveling.

Crocheting truly is a straightforward hobby to pick up, but there are a few basic stitches to master before embarking on a project. Once you learn these stitches, you will be able to make almost anything. It's one of the best-kept secrets of crochet: anything you wish to make will use only a few basic stitches or variations of those stitches. When you combine them in different ways, you can create intricate patterns that will have people in awe of your talent, while you just smirk, knowing how simple it was!

Remember that practice makes perfect in everything, especially in crocheting. Though the stitches are simple, you'll have to perfect your technique for creating the right amount of tension in your yarn. If your first few stitches are a bit wonky, don't give up! With practice and small adjustments, you'll soon be producing quality pieces that you will be proud to show to others!

The most basic technique you must learn is how to hold your hook and yarn. There are several ways deemed to be correct, and I'll show you each of them. But remember that the only thing that truly matters is that you are able to hold the hook, hold the yarn, and move them around to be able to actually create something!

The easiest yarn to learn with will be any cheap yarn that you can find in any store — Wal-Mart has a "Mainstay" brand, which is what I will be using in the pictures below. The easiest hook to begin learning on is the "I/9" one. So without further ado:

Holding the Yarn

First, run your yarn under your pinky finger (1). Then run the yarn over your ring and middle finger (2).

1. Run the yarn over your pinky finger:

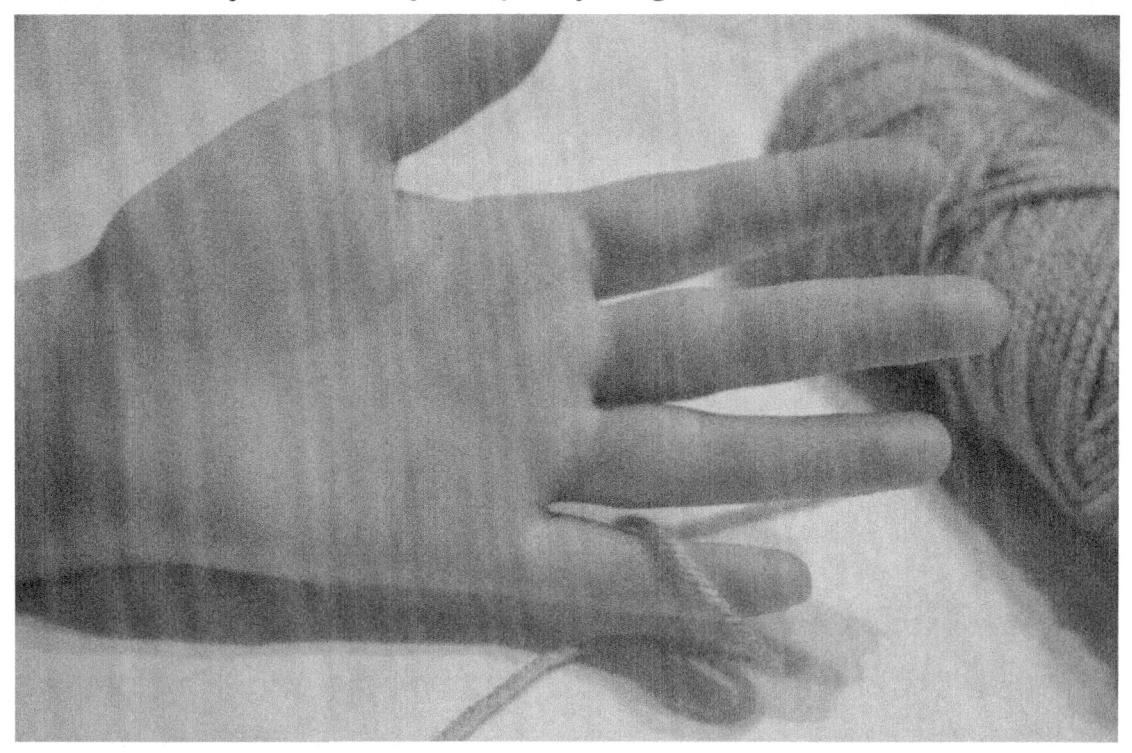

2. Under your next two fingers:
3. And over your pointer finger:

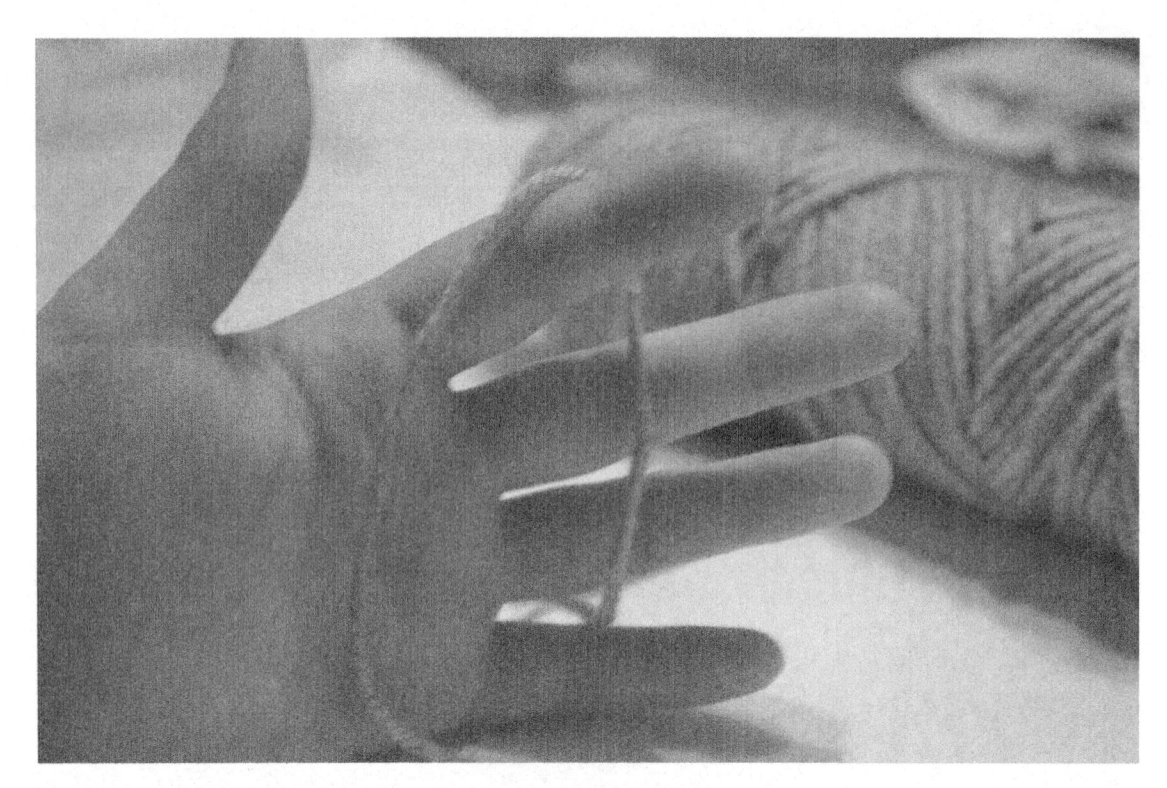

Then you will hold your project with your middle finger and thumb as you work.

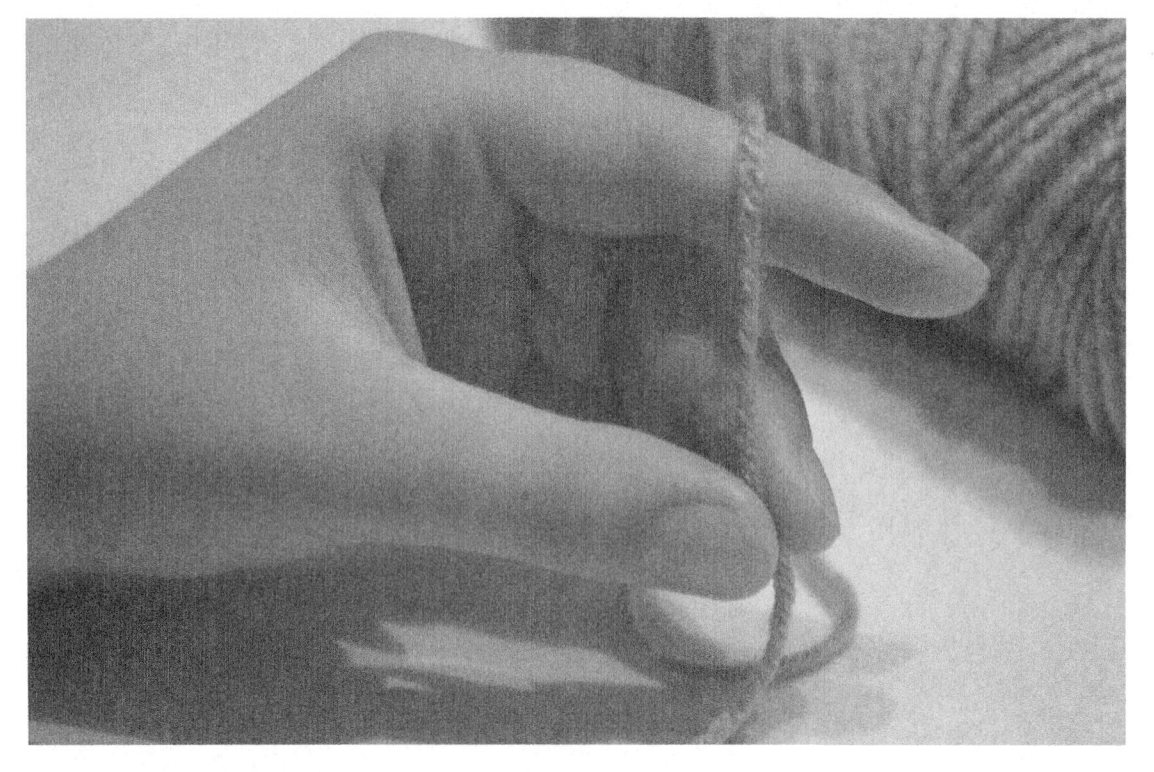

Holding the Hook:

There are two ways to hold the hook. The first is to hold it like a butter knife:

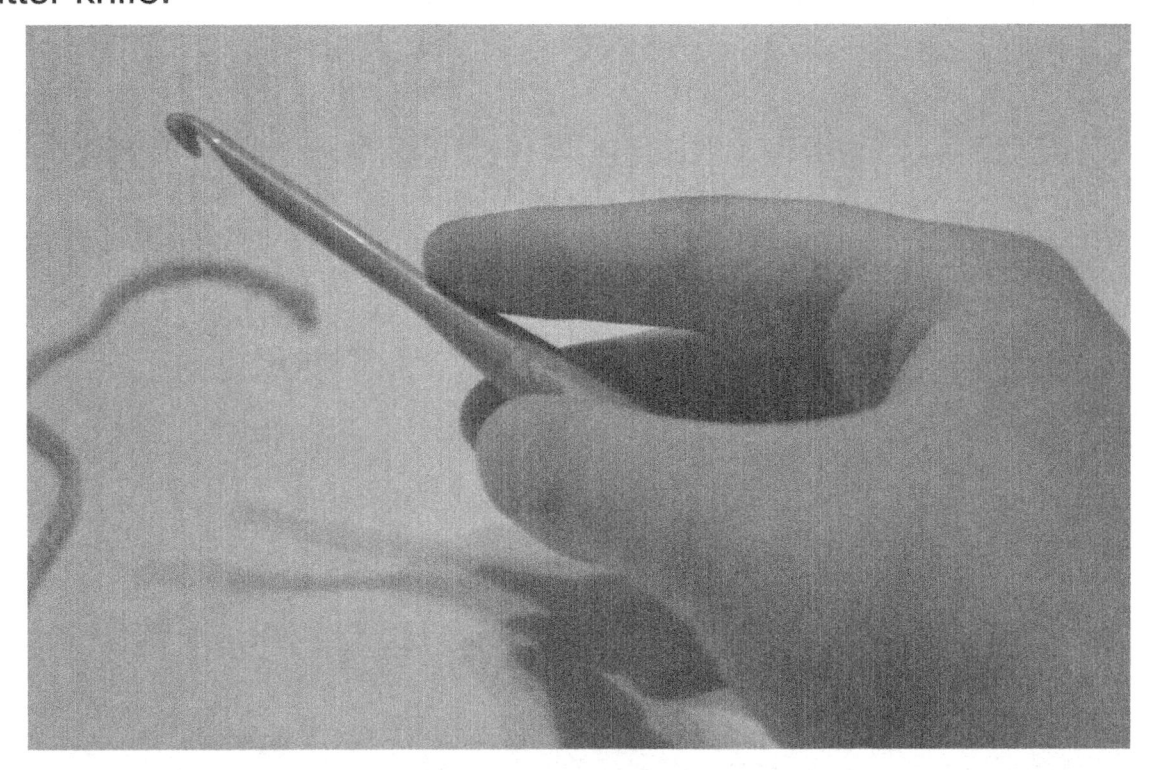

And the second way is to hold it like a pencil:

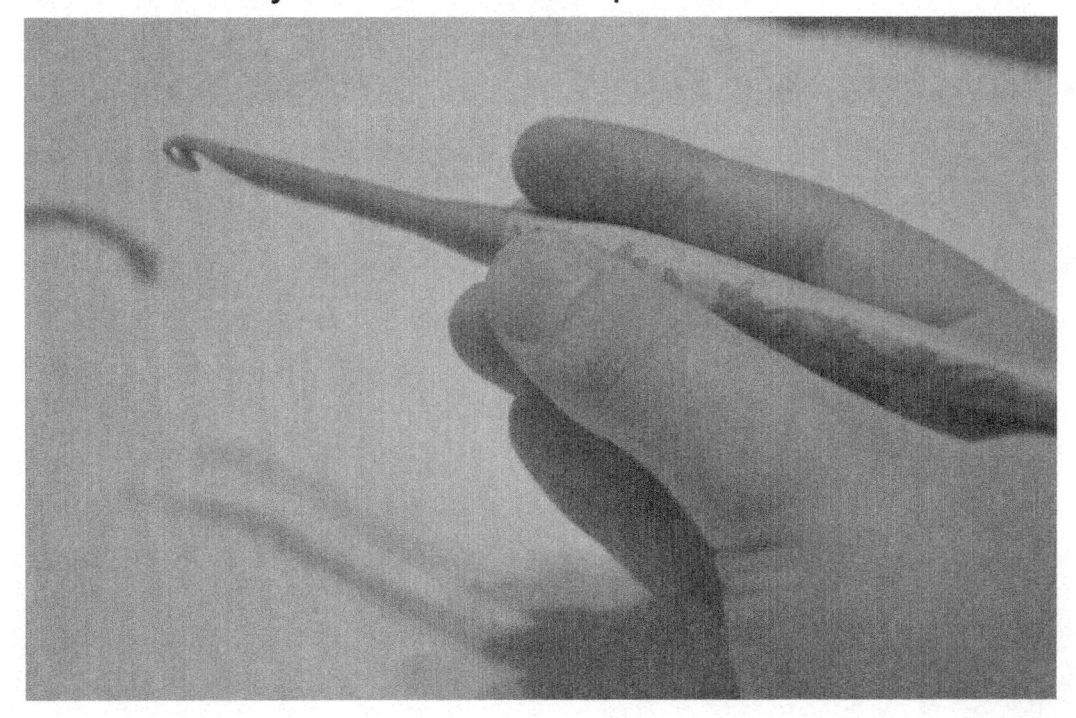

Now that we have the basics out of the way, we can actually start to learn to use them! To begin with, we need to attach the yarn to the hook with a **slip knot.** This is how every single piece will start. Form a loop of yarn:

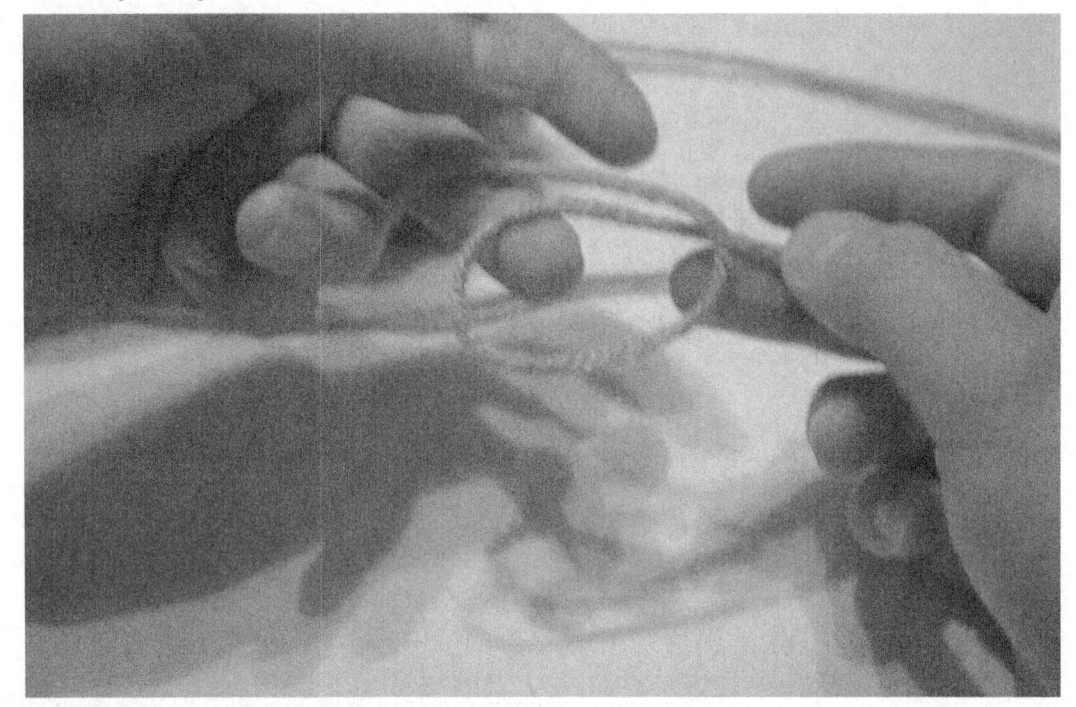

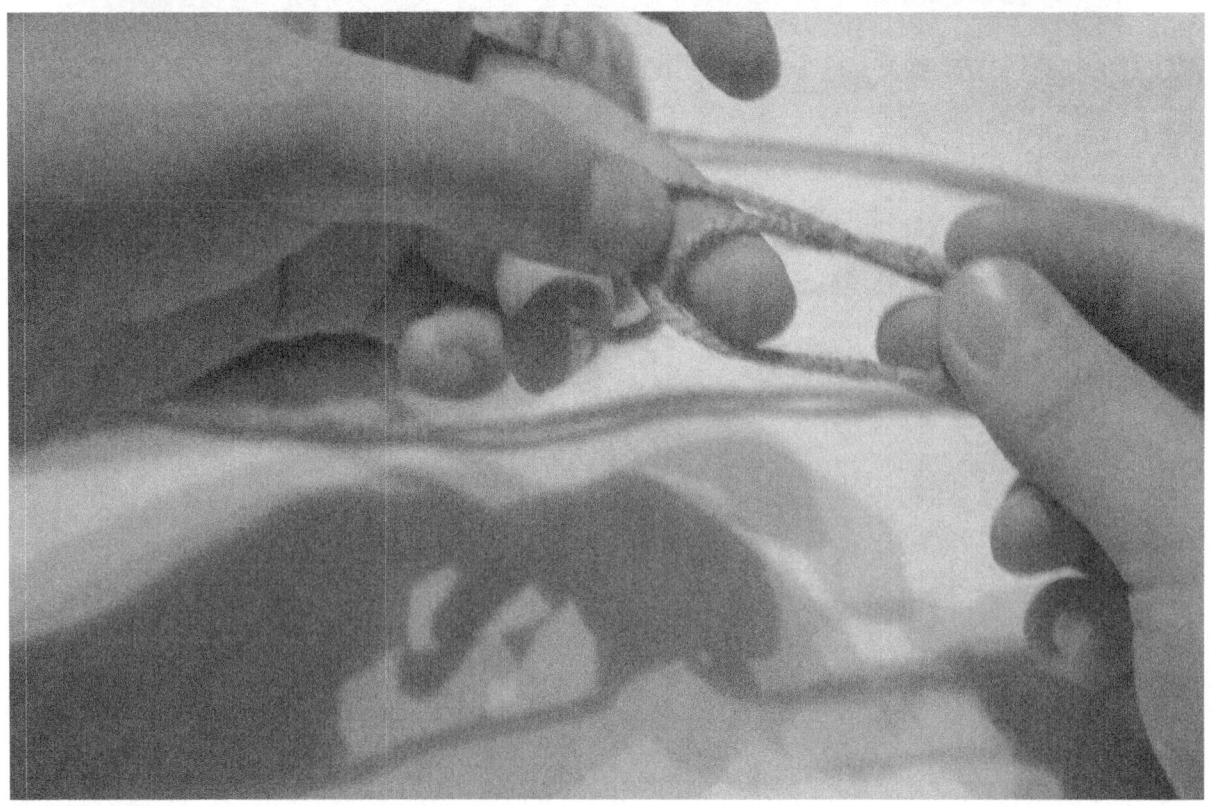

With the tail running behind the center of the loop:

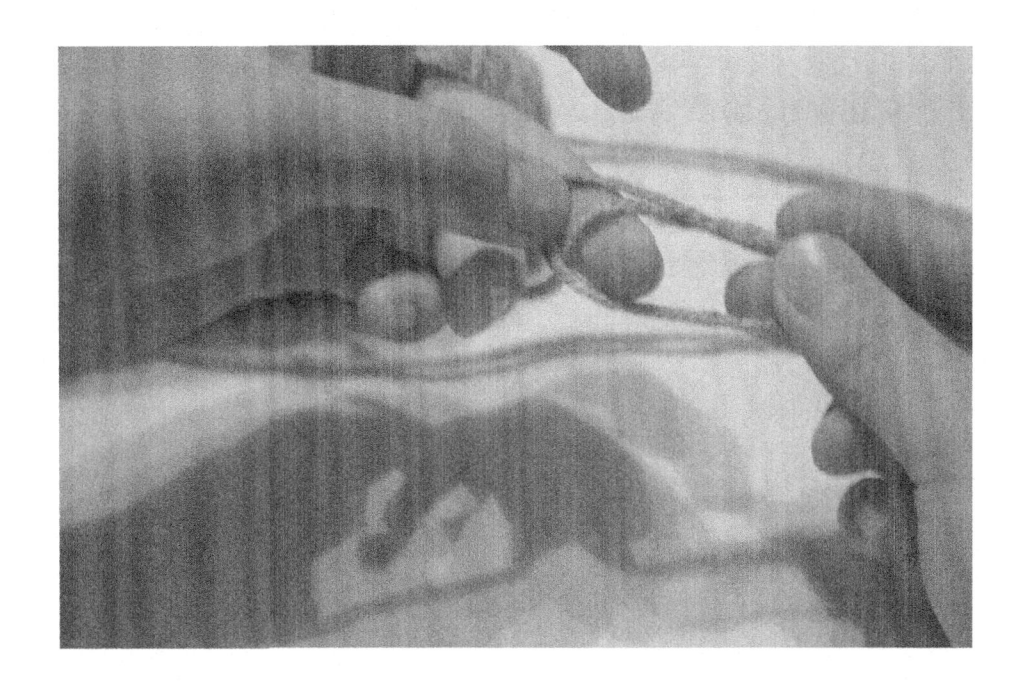

Pick up that tail piece with the hook:

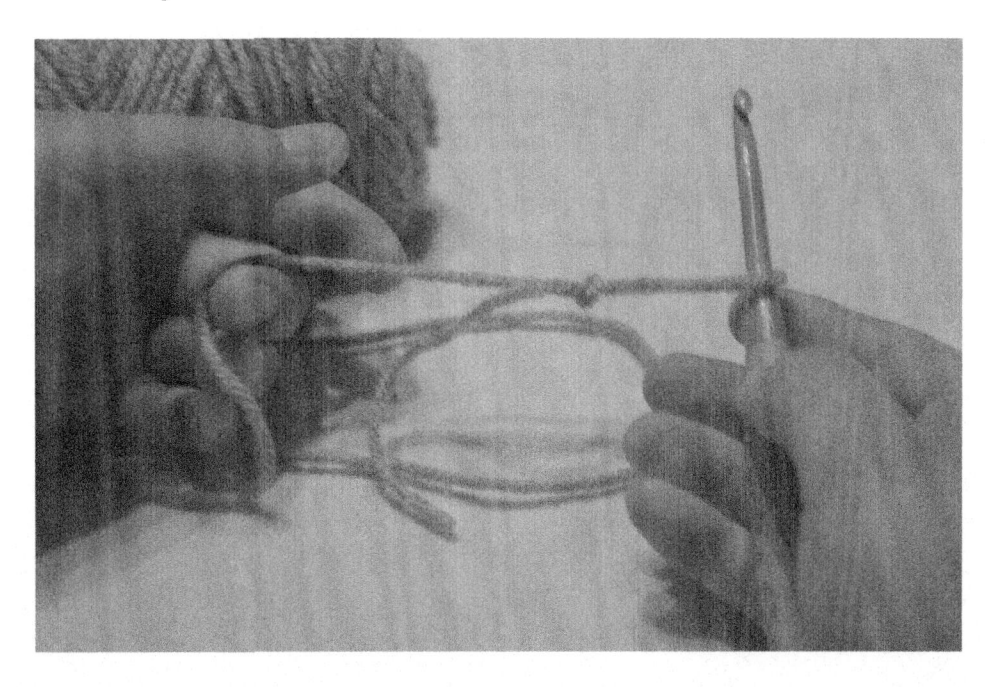

Snug the yarn to the crochet hook, and you're ready to start! Make sure that when you start your stitches, you use the yarn that is coming from your skein and not the tail, or else you'll have to start back from square one.

The first stitch you will need to learn for crochet is a **chain stitch.** The chain stitch will form the base for every pattern you create, so it is, without a doubt, the most important stitch you will learn.

To make the chain, you hold the hook and the yarn as you've already been shown, like this:

Grab the working yarn (not the tail!) with the hook:

Pull the yarn through the loop already on the hook — you have now completed your first chain!

Repeat these steps until you have reached the number of chains specified in your pattern. When working stitches into your initial chain, you will insert the hook between the top two loops and the bottom one.

Single Crochet Stitch

The single crochet stitch is simply a single loop of thread that forms a single knot. Single crochet stitches will create a dense, heavy fabric, perfect or warm-weather garments.

To work the single crochet stitch, insert your hook through the stitch, or chain of the previous round:

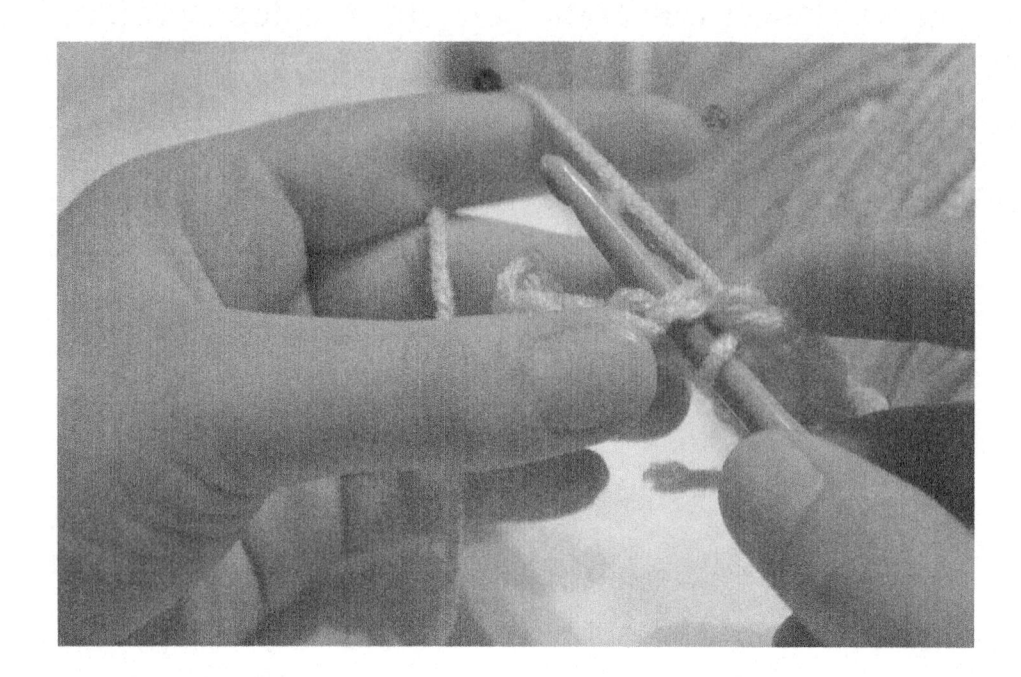

Hook the working yarn with the hook, and pull it through the stitch — you should now have two loops on your hook:

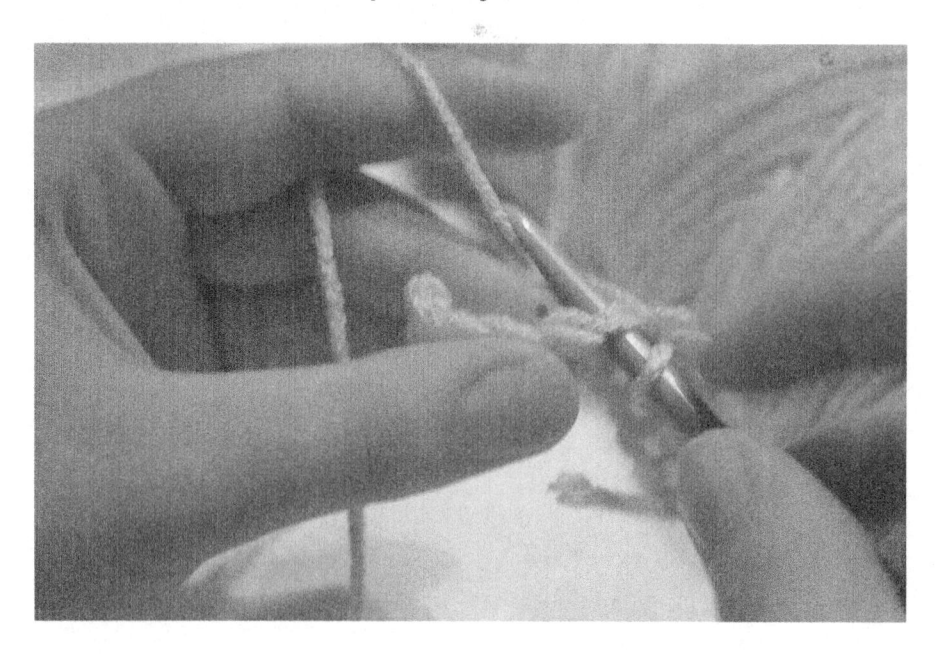

Hook the yarn once more, and pull it through both loops on the hook:

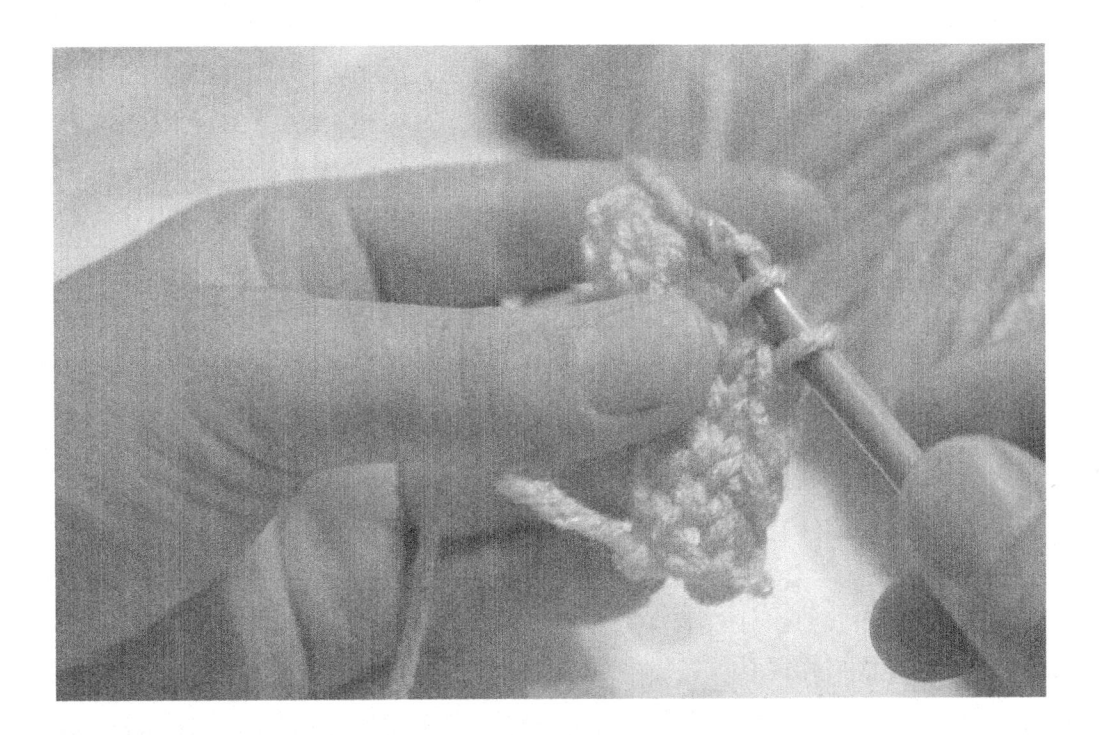

You have now completed your first single crochet stitch! Continue to practice this stitch until you can uniformly work them with tension that is consistent.

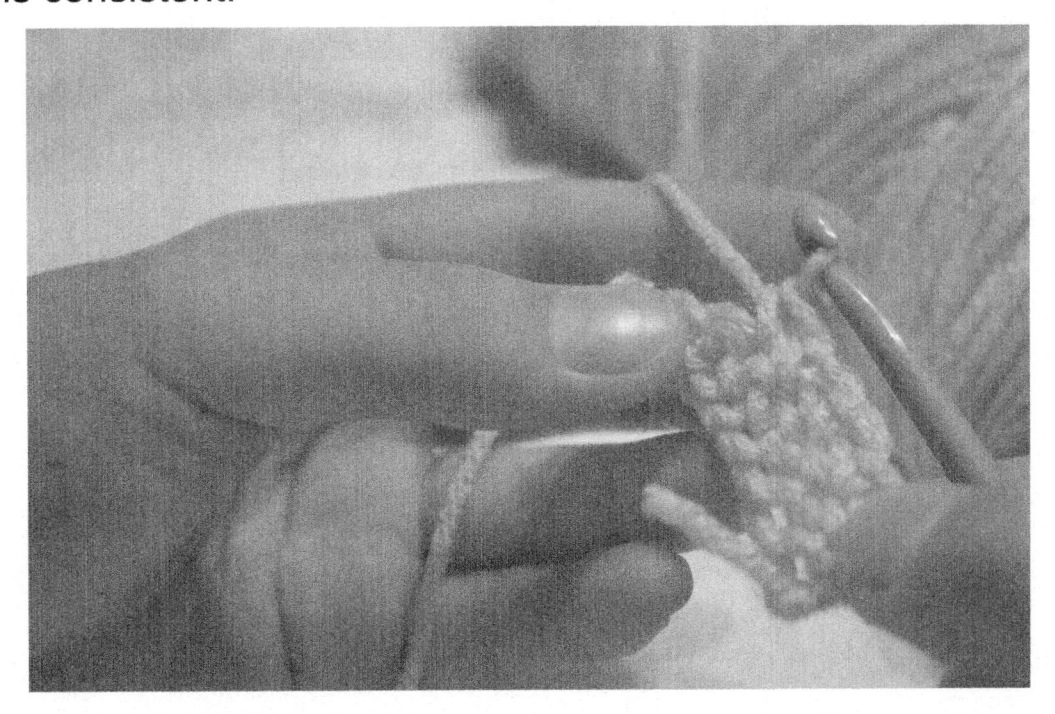

A note about the tension of the yarn:

As you continue to work the stitches, you may realize that some stitches take a bit of work to push the hook through, and at times the hook just slips right in, as if the stitch is too big for the hook. At other times the hook fits into the stitch like a glove: that is the perfect tension.

The tension — or tightness — of the stitch depends on how you are holding your yarn with your pinky. If you are holding it too tightly, and aren't pulling up a big enough loop into the beginning of the stitch, then your stitches are going to be too tight, until the hook isn't even able to get into the stitch anymore.

On the other hand, if you are letting the yarn just slide through your fingers without giving any resistance at all, then the loops you pull up are going to be big and, well, loopy, keeping you from seeing any stitch definition at all.

One way to keep the stitch tension right is to provide a bit of resistance to the yarn between your pinky and the other fingers. Not too much, but don't let it just pull easily, either. One way to fix the loops being too small or big is to slide the loop of yarn up the shaft of the hook, just a little bit, before moving forward with your stitches.

This will keep the loops consistent, and eventually, it will become second nature to you!

Half Double Crochet Stitch

The half double crochet stitch is called this because it is half the size of the regular double crochet stitch. This stitch is not as dense as the single crochet stitch, but it is also not quite as loose as the double crochet. This stitch is used many times to create a compact, yet flexible fabric, and it is used to shape garments.

Wrap your yarn around the hook:

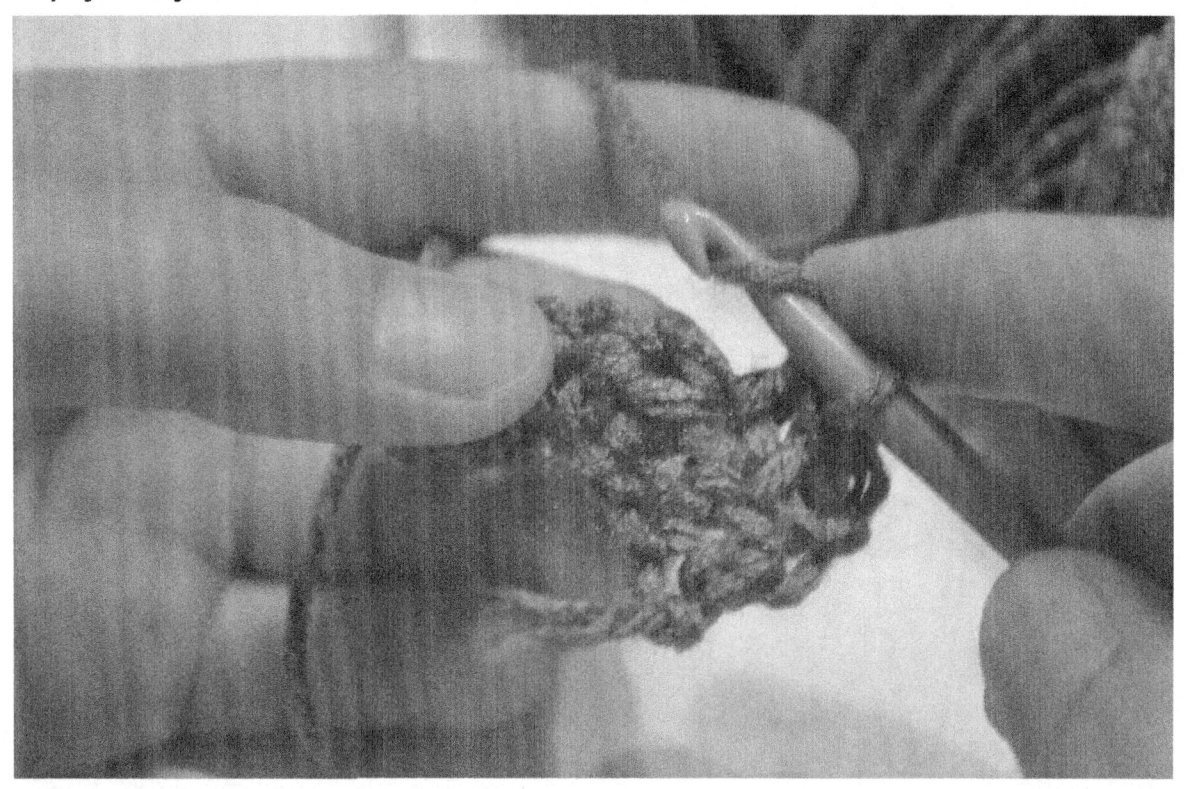

Insert the hook into the stitch:

Use the hook to grab the yarn and pull it through the stitch. You should now have three loops of yarn on your hook.

Grab the yarn with the hook again and pull it through all three loops on the hook.

Double Crochet Stitch

This stitch is similar to the half double crochet stitch. It produces an open, almost lacy fabric, and works up quickly.

Start the same way as you would with the half double crochet stitch: wrap the yarn around your hook . . .

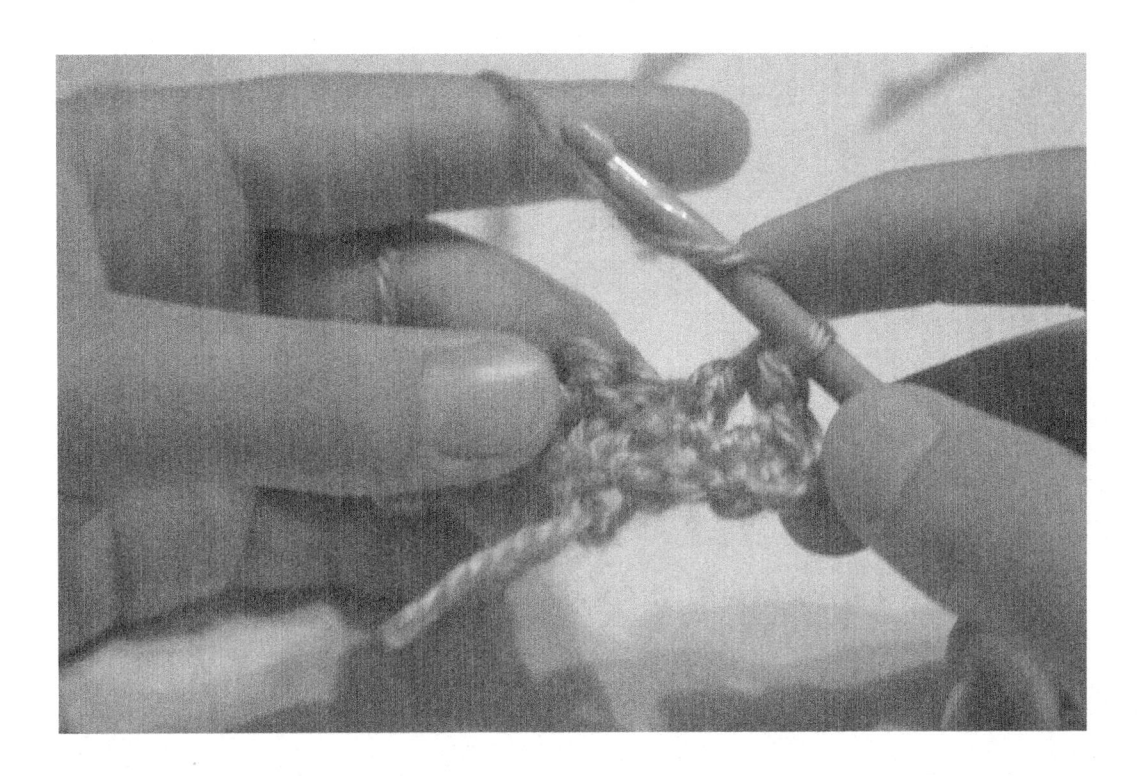

And insert it into the stitch. Grab the yarn and pull it through the stitch. You now have three loops on the hook.

Now hook the yarn and pull it through *only the first two loops on the hook.* You should still have two loops on the hook.

Grab the yarn once more, and pull it through the last two loops left on the hook.

Practice this stitch, and all of these until the stitches are uniformed, even, and smooth.

Slip Stitch

This last stitch is one that is used for shaping and for joining rounds, or for edging a finished piece. It is the shortest stitch, and a piece of fabric completed entirely from slip stitches would be very thick, and it would take a while to see any progress.

Put your hook into the stitch specified in the pattern.

Hook the yarn and pull it through both the stitch and the loop already on the hook.

And there you have it — the basic stitches you need to complete any project!

Using a Pattern

*Crochetsomnia: (crochet - som - nia), noun;
the inability to get enough sleep because you are crocheting just one more row. . .*

Now that you know the basic stitches that you need to start a project, you may realize just how confusing a written crochet pattern can be. We crocheters use a secret code to refer to our stitches, pattern counts, and so on. Once you get the hang of reading patterns, though, it's easy to get to work on a project!

A good pattern will have stitch counts, tell you what hook size you need, and inform you as to what kind of yarn and how much is required for the project. An excellent pattern will have pictures and helpful hints along the way.

When using a pattern, you will either work in rows or in rounds. When working rows, you will work the piece back and forth, turning at each end. Most patterns will call for a few turning chains, depending on what stitch you are using, and most patterns will have you count those turning chains as a single stitch for the purposes of the pattern.

When working rows, it is important to make sure you work all the way to the end and work one last stitch in the top turning chain of the previous row. If you notice your work slanting in on the sides, it's because you're inadvertently skipping the last stitch, which is actually the turning chains. Make sure you are working those!

When working in the round, you will use a stitch marker to hold your place at the beginning of the round. As you come back to the beginning, marked by your stitch marker is, you take off the stitch marker, work the stitch, and put it back on the stitch you just worked. You work the item just as the name implies: around and around and around. There are projects involving both of these techniques in this book, and I'll walk you through them step by step.

A note about the turning chain:

When working in rows, most patterns will utilize what is called a "turning chain," and it is generally counted as the first stitch in your next row. There's a formula to this, and once you learn it, you'll be all set.

First, turn your work. Either way will work, but I find it more natural for myself to turn it counter-clockwise.

Now chain the specified amount. Typically, you work:

- One turning chain for single crochet stitches
- Two turning chains for half double crochet stitches
- Three turning chains for double crochet stitches.

These chains are equal to the height of the actual stitch. There are more advanced ways and techniques, but this is the most commonly used way to turn a piece. After working a turning chain, start working in the stitch directly after the chain, not the stitch the chain is on top of!

Gauge and Swatches

The gauge of a pattern tells you how many stitches with a particular sized hook will equal how many inches. If your gauge is off, try upping your hook size or choosing a smaller hook to hit the gauge.

The projects in this book don't have a gauge noted — for these particular patterns, the gauge isn't necessary. But it is imperative when working a sweater, a pair of slippers, a hat, or any other size-specific pattern. If your gauge is off, the pattern measurements will be off too, and the item will end up not fitting properly.

Always make sure you work the swatch to the size specified in the pattern to get gauge.

Reading the Pattern

As you read through the pattern, you may notice an odd mixture of numbers and letters. The letters are abbreviations of certain stitches, and the numbers are your stitch count. In an effort to make learning easier for you, so you can get on to the fun of creating things, I have chosen not to use abbreviations. Eventually, you will have to learn and deal with the abbreviated lingo of crochet — but it is easy to learn, and a good pattern will have a guide explaining the abbreviations the designer chose to use.

The straightforward, simple abbreviations that rarely change are as follows:

- **Ch.** — Chain
- **SC** — Single Crochet
- **HDC** — Half Double Crochet
- **DC** — Double Crochet
- **SS (or SL ST)** — Slip Stitch

Now, just follow the pattern as it is written. If you come to a really confusing part that you simply don't understand, just follow the directions, as slowly as you can. You will find, nine times out of ten, that the problem is cleared up just by working through it. If it helps, mark each stitch as you complete it so you know exactly which stitch you are working next.

When you finish a piece, you will want to cut the yarn holding the work to the skein, making sure to leave about 5 inches. Pull the loop on the crochet hook to make it large, and pull the tail through the loop, pulling it tight to create a knot. Use a crochet hook or a yarn needle to weave the end into the fabric of the crochet piece.

Now, are you ready to create some stunning pieces of work?

Patterns
Woven Together Afghan

A timeless pattern that gives you the creativity to combine colors of yarn to your heart's delight! Mix and match several colors, or one or two, to provide you with a unique, one-of-a-kind project that will have others marveling in awe! Although it looks complicated, this is a great first project, as you are able to practice the basic stitches. By the end of this, you will have it mastered!

Supplies Needed

- Size I/9 (5.5mm) crochet hook

Part 1:

- 1, 500 yards of DK weight yarn — mix and match colors. (I used Red Heart Super Saver Jumbo — 2 skeins. Colorway Aran)

Part 2:

- 1, 490 yards of DK weight yarn — mix and match colors. (I used Redheart Super Saver, color way Dusty Grey and Mainstay, color way)

Border:

- 400 yards of DK weight yarn — mix and match colors. (I used the same colors from part 2)

Pattern

Part 1

Row 1: Chain 145.

Double crochet in the 3rd chain from the hook and in each chain across. Turn.

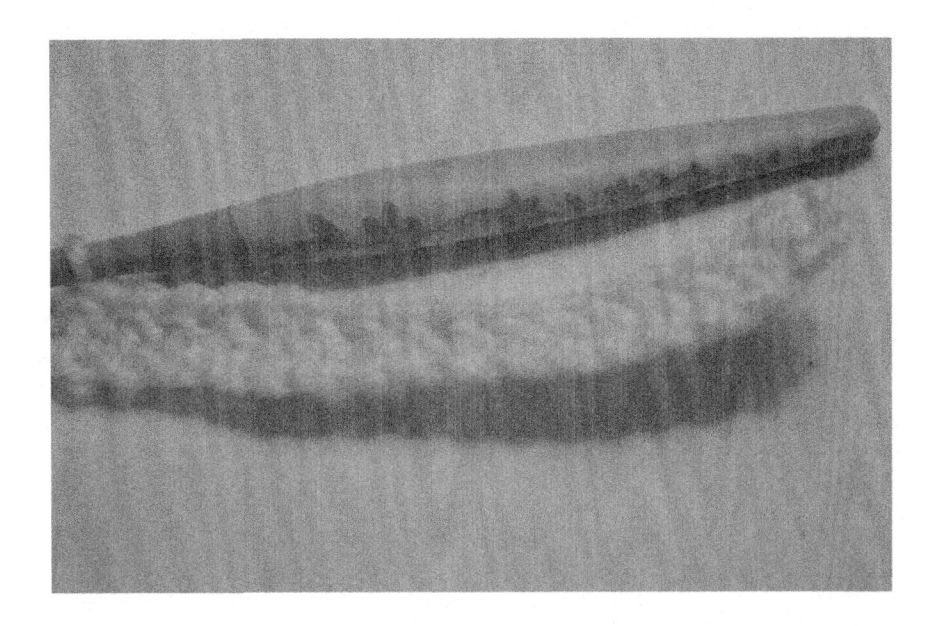

Row 2: Chain 3.

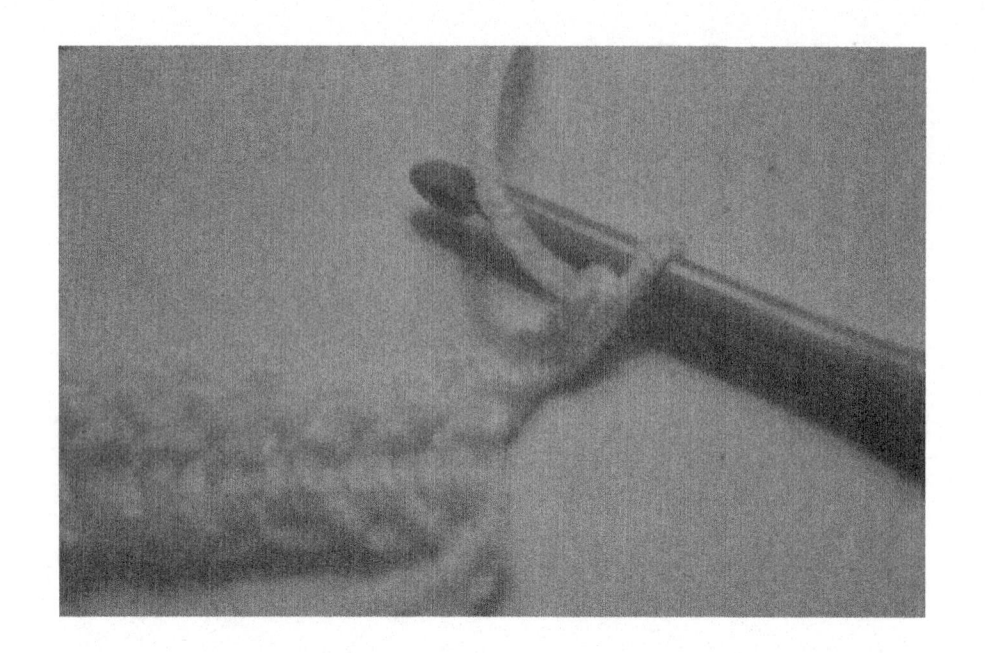

Double crochet in each stitch across. Turn.

Repeat row 2 until you have completed 10 total rows. Fasten off. You will need to complete a total of 9 of these.

Part 2

Row 1: Chain 117. Double crochet in 3rd chain from hook and in each chain across. Turn.

Row 2: Chain 3. Double crochet in each stitch across. Turn.

Repeat two 2 or a total of 10 rows. Fasten off. You will need to complete 11 of these in total — I made 5 one color and 6 another.

Assembling

Take your strips from part 1 and lay them out on a flat surface — a table or a bed or just the floor. Lay them out long sides together, right next to each other.

Take the strips from Part 2 and weave them in and out of the strips from Part 1, snugging them together. As you go, use clothespins or binder clips to hold the edges together.

60

Take a yarn needle and whichever color yarn you would like to tie the blanket together. Starting with a long length of yarn, go through two opposite corners of the same color.

Tie in a simple knot, and cut, leaving about 2-inch tails. Now go through the opposite corners, tie, and leave a 2-inch tail.

Do this all over the blanket — this took a while, so put on music you like and get to it.

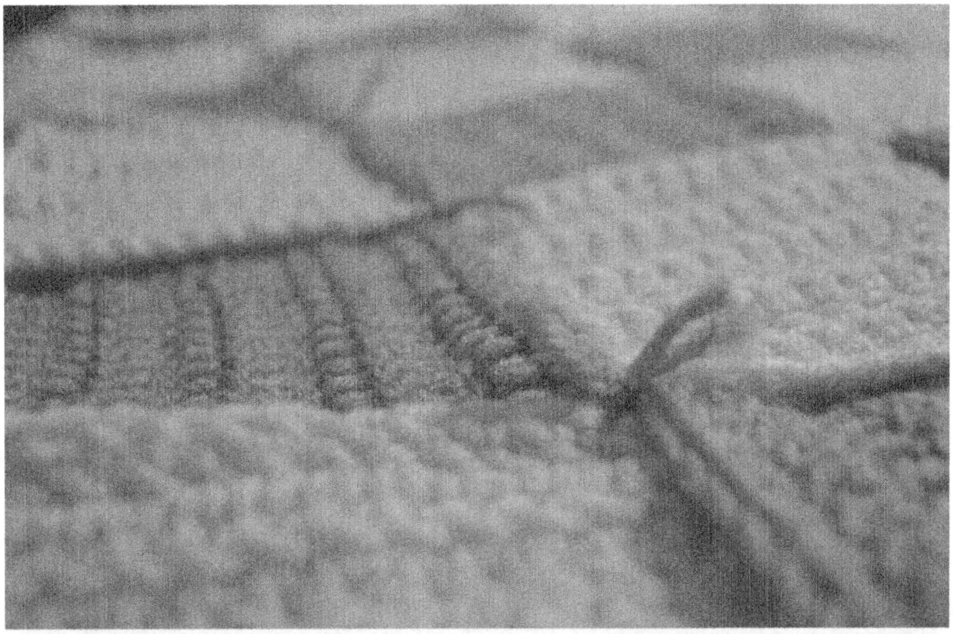

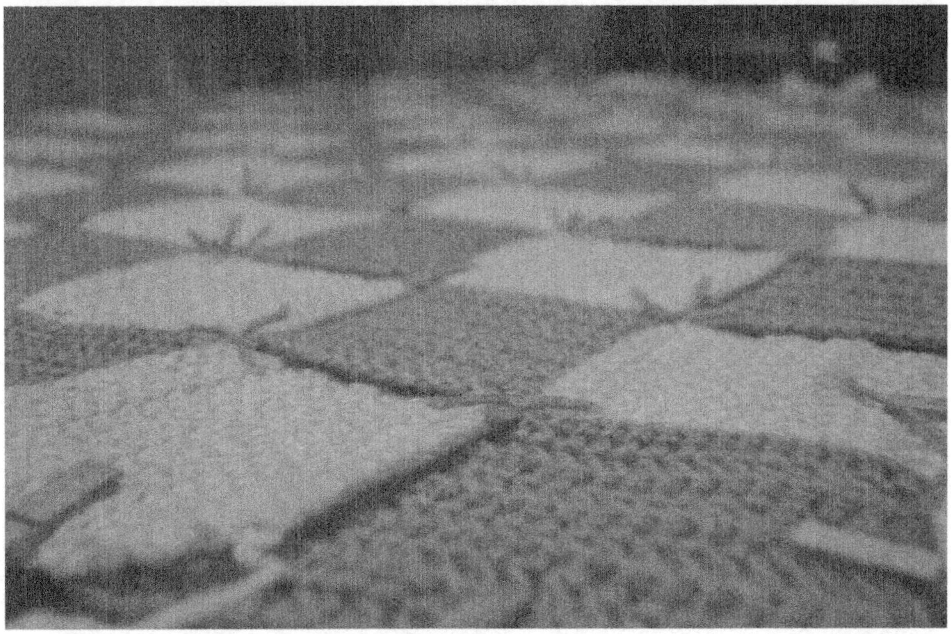

Border

Use whichever color you'd like and, with the right side of the blanket facing you, start single crocheting around the edge, starting anywhere.

Place 3 stitches in each corner:

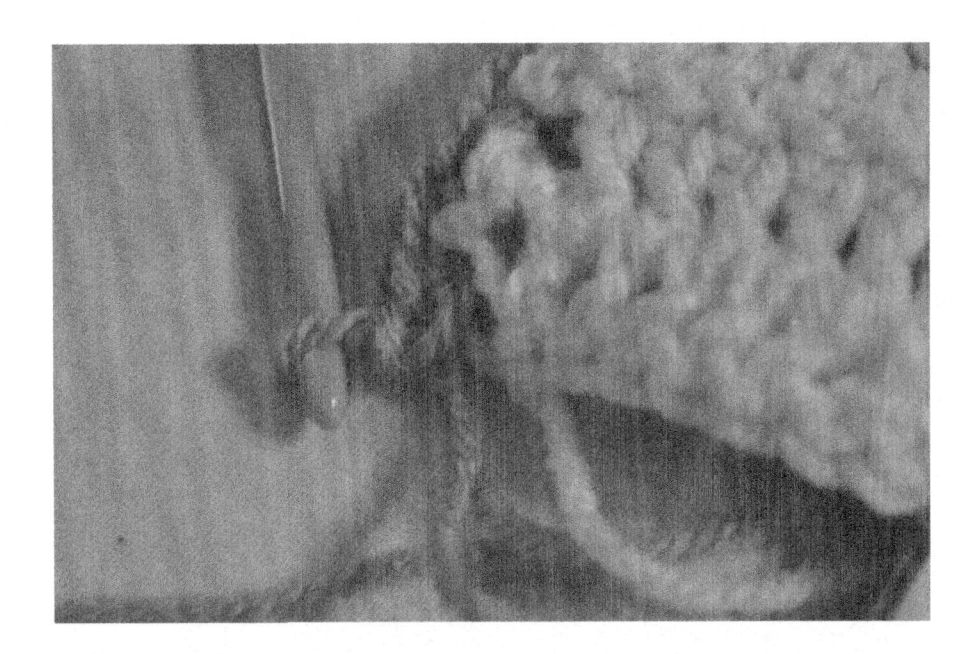

Remove the clothespins/binder clips as you get to them. Make sure the edges match up on both sides. Join with a slip stitch in the first stitch made to finish the initial border.

Half double crochet 5 rows around the blanket, placing 3 stitches in each corner stitch.

Fasten off and cut yarn.

Using a different color, attach the yarn at any point of the border.

Chain 3.

In the same stitch, yarn over, draw up a loop, draw yarn through 2 loops, yarn over, draw up a loop, draw yarn through 2 loops — there should now be 3 loops on the hook. Yarn over and draw through all loops on hook.

*Chain 1. Skip the next stitch. In the next, half double crochet, yarn over, insert hook in stitch, draw up a loop yarn over and pull yarn through 2 loops:

Yarn over, insert hook into the same stitch, draw up a loop, yarn over and pull through 2 loops:

Yarn over, insert hook into the same stitch, draw up a loop, yarn over and pull through 2 loops. There should now be 4 loops on the hook.

Yarn over and pull through all loops. **Cluster Stitch made.**

Repeat the cluster stitch starting at the * .

Work until you reach the end of the round, placing 2 cluster stitches into each corner.

Fasten off and cut the yarn, leaving 5 inches of tail.

Attach the first color of the border in any stitch of the edge, with the right side facing you.

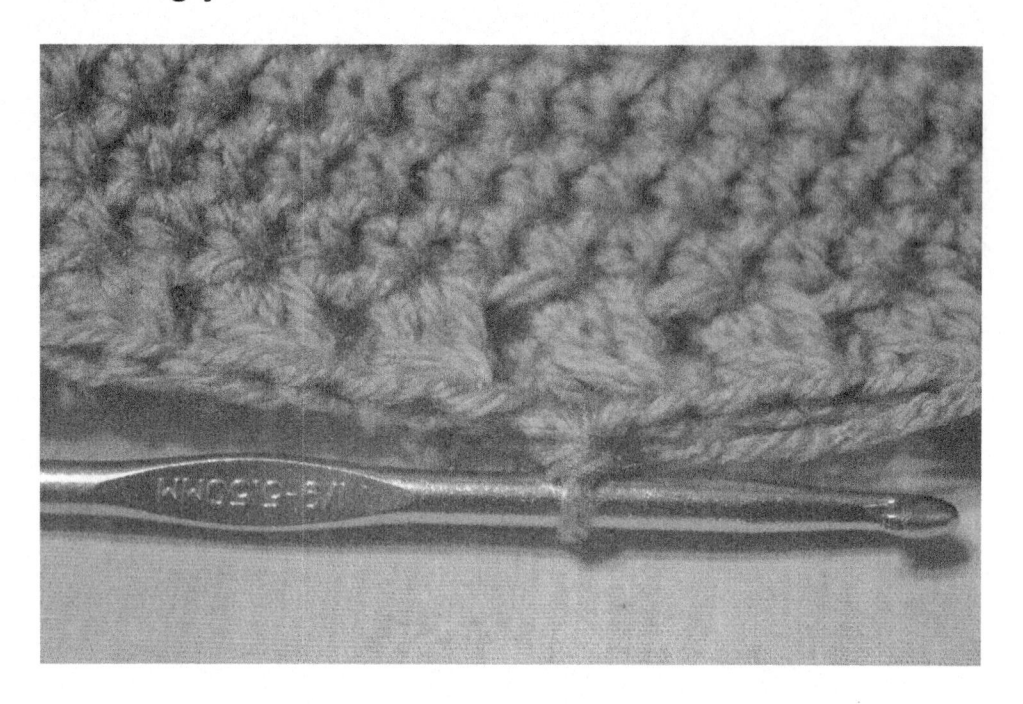

Chain 2.

Half double crochet in the same stitch, (half double crochet in chain 1 space, half double crochet in next stitch) around.

Place three stitches in each chain 1 space of the corner. Join with a slip stitch at the end.

Fasten off and weave in ends.

Carry-All Tote Bag

This simple bag is perfect for a wide variety of uses! The cotton yarn gives the fabric of the bag a lot of give, making it perfect to use for shopping at farmer's markets, toting things for a picnic, or holding your latest project and keeping all that yarn in one place! It works up quickly and makes the perfect gift.

Supplies Needed

206 yards of size 4/worsted weight cotton yarn (I used "I Love this Cotton!" — 2 skeins — from Hobby Lobby; color way: Spunky.)

Size I/9 (5.5mm) crochet hook

Stitch Marker

Pattern Notes

This piece will be worked in the round, starting from the bottom of the bag and working up. Use a stitch marker to mark the first stitch of each round, moving the marker as you go.

The chains used at the beginning of each round are counted as the first pitch throughout unless otherwise noted.

Pattern

Round 1: Chain three.

Half double crochet 7 times into the 3rd stitch from the hook.

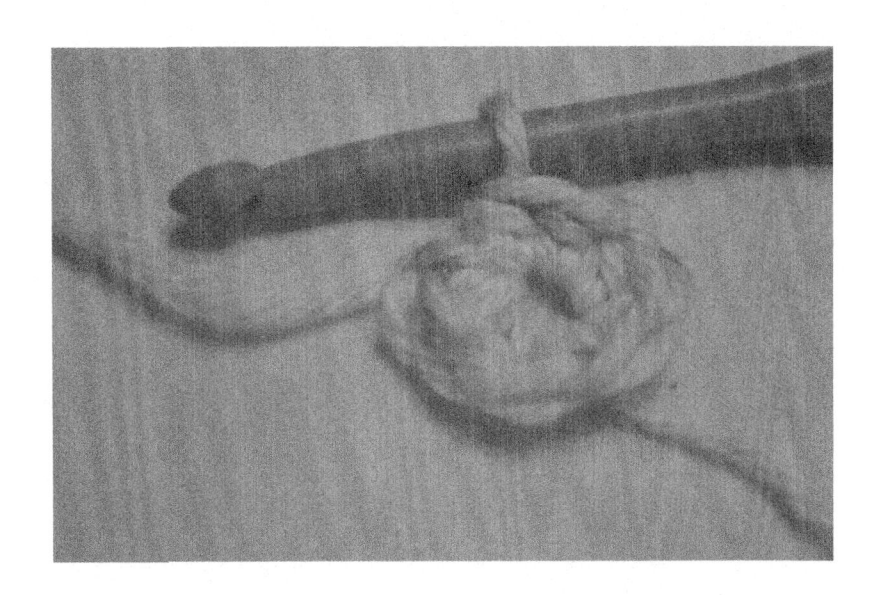

Join to top of the first chain with a slip stitch — 8 half double crochets.

Round 2: Chain 2.

Half double crochet in the same stitch.

2 half double crochet in each stitch around. Join with a slip stitch to top of first chain — 16 stitches. Place your marker to mark the beginning and end of the round.

Round 3: Chain 2. Work (2 half double crochet in next stitch, one half double in next stitch) around.

Join at the top of the first chain — 24 stitches.

Round 4: Chain 2. Work (2 half double crochet in next stitch, 1 half double crochet in next two stitches) around. Join to top of first chain — 32 stitches.

Round 5: Chain 2. Work (2 half double crochet in next stitch, 1 half double crochet in next three stitches) around. Join in top of first chain — 40 stitches.

Round 6: Chain 2. Work (2 half double crochet in next stitch, 1 half double crochet in next four stitches) around. Join in top of first chain — 48 stitches.

Round 7: Chain 2. Work (2 half double crochet in next stitch, 1 half double crochet in next 5 stitches) around. Join in the top first chain - 56 stitches.

Round 8: Chain 2. Work (2 half double crochet in next stitch, 1 half double crochet in next 6 stitches) around. Join in top of first chain —64 stitches.

Round 9: Chain 2. Work (2 half double crochet in next stitch, 1 half double crochet in next 7 stitches) around. Join in top of first chain —72 stitches.

Round 10: Chain 2. Work (2 half double crochet in next stitch, 1 half double crochet in next 8 stitches) around. Join in top of first chain —80 stitches.

Round 11: Chain 2. Work (2 half double crochet in next stitch, 1 half double crochet in next 9 stitches) around. Join in top of first chain —88 stitches.

Round 12: Chain 2. Work (2 half double crochet in next stitch, 1 half double crochet in next 10 stitches) around. Join in top of the first chain —96 stitches.

Round 13: Chain 3. Double crochet in the same space.

(1 double crochet in next 11 stitches, 2 double crochet in next stitch) around. Join in top of chain three — remove marker.

Round 14: Chain 4. Work (skip the next stitch, double crochet in the next stitch, chain 1) around. Join in top of chain 3 — 104 stitches.

85

Round 15: Chain 4. Work (skip the next chain 1 space, double crochet in next double crochet, chain 1) around. Join in top of chain 3.

Round 16: Chain 4. Work (skip the next chain 1 space, double crochet in next double crochet, chain 1) around. Join in top of chain 3.

Round 17: Chain 4. (skip the next chain 1 space, double crochet in next double crochet, chain 1) 13 times; double crochet, chain 1, double crochet) in next stitch

(chain 1, skip the next chain 1 space, double crochet in next double crochet) 13 times; chain 1, (double crochet, chain 1, double crochet) in next stitch; (chain 1, skip the next chain 1 space, double crochet in next double crochet)13 times; chain 1, (double crochet, chain 1, double crochet) in next stitch; (chain 1, skip the next chain 1 space, double crochet in next double crochet) 13 times; chain 1, (double crochet, chain 1, double crochet) in next stitch; chain 1, join in top of chain 3.

Round 18: Chain 4. Work (double crochet in next double crochet, chain 1) around. Join in top of chain 3.

Round 19: Chain 3. Work (1 double crochet in chain 1 space, 1 double crochet in next double crochet) around. Join in top of chain 3 space.

Round 20: Chain 3. Double crochet in each double crochet around.

Round 21: Chain 4. Work (skip the next stitch, double crochet in the next stitch, chain 1) around. Join in top of chain 3.

Round 22: Chain 4. (skip the next chain 1 space, double crochet in next double crochet, chain 1) 14 times; double crochet, chain 1, double crochet) in next stitch; (chain 1, skip the next chain 1 space, double crochet in next double crochet) 14 times; chain 1, (double crochet, chain 1, double crochet) in next stitch; (chain 1, skip the next chain 1 space, double crochet in next double crochet)14 times; chain 1, (double crochet, chain 1, double crochet) in next stitch; (chain 1, skip the next chain 1 space, double crochet in next double crochet) 14 times; chain 1, (double crochet, chain 1, double crochet) in next stitch; chain 1, join in top of chain 3.

Round 23: Chain 4. Work (skip the next chain 1 space, double crochet in next double crochet, chain 1) around. Join in top of chain 3.

Round 24: Chain 4. Work (skip the next chain 1 space, double crochet in next double crochet, chain 1) around. Join in top of chain 3.

Round 25: Chain 4. Work (skip the next chain 1 space, double crochet in next double crochet, chain 1) around. Join in top of chain 3.

Round 26: Chain 3. Work (1 double crochet in chain 1 space, 1 double crochet in next double crochet) around. Join in top of chain 3 space.

Round 27: Chain 3. Double crochet in next 14 stitches, double crochet the next two stitches together.

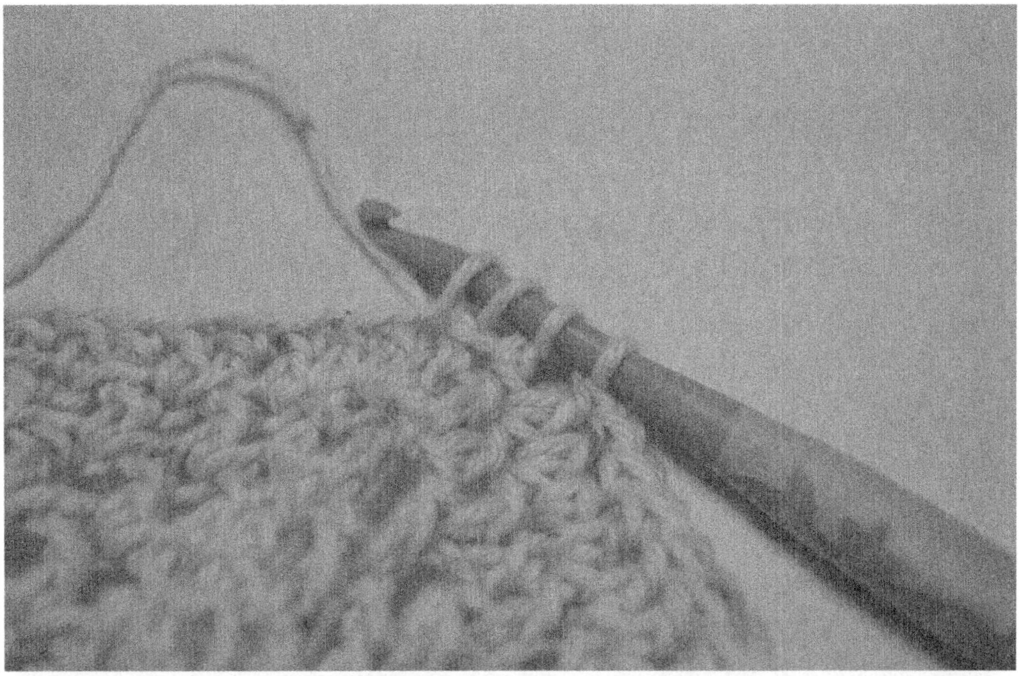

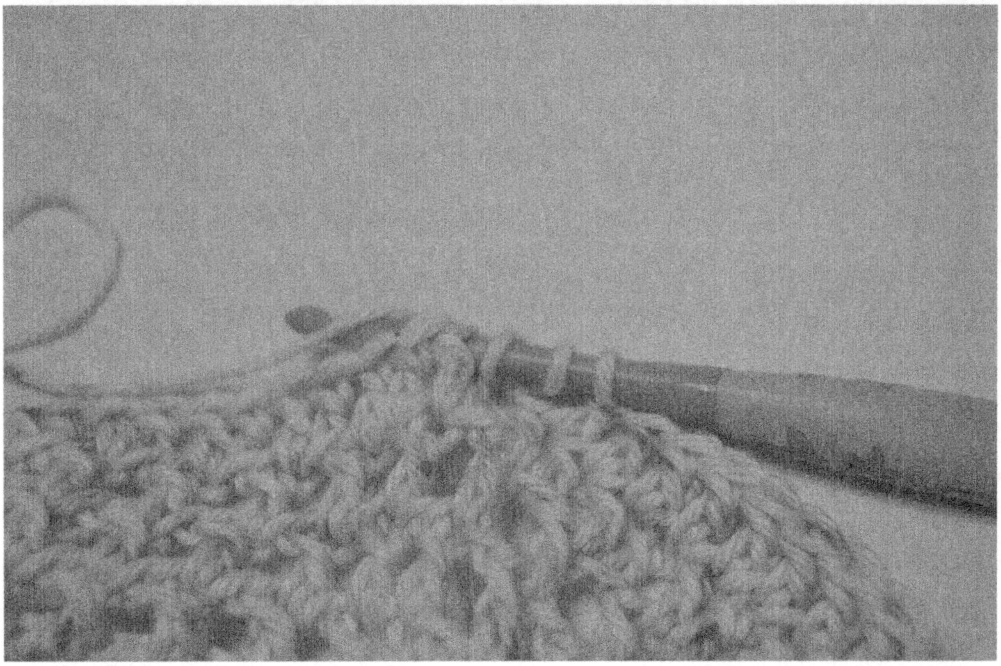

(Double crochet in next 15 stitches, double crochet 2 together) around. Double crochet to last 2 stitches, double crochet the last 2 stitches together. Join to top of chain 3 — 120 stitches.

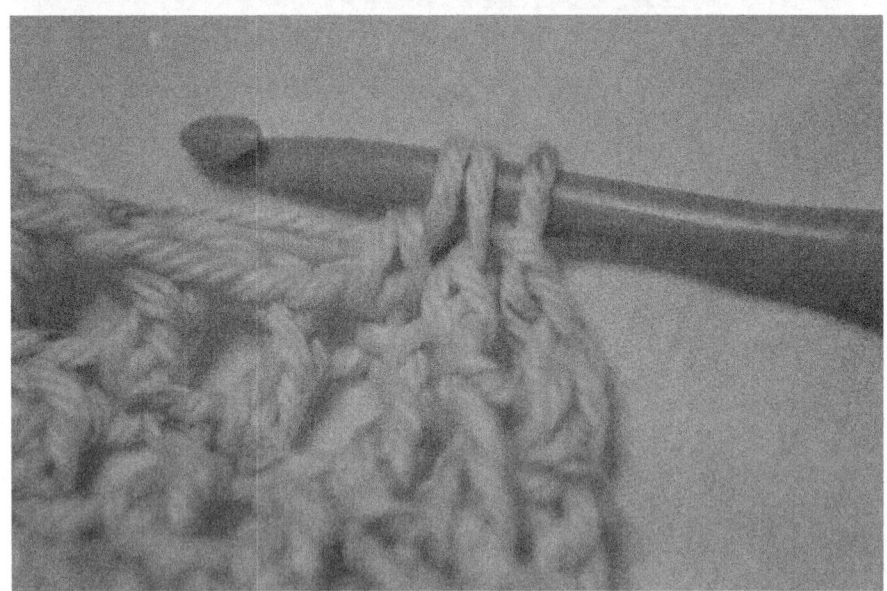

Round 28: Chain 4. Work (skip the next stitch, double crochet in the next stitch, chain 1) around. Join in top of chain 3.

Round 29: Chain 4. Work (skip the next chain 1 space, double crochet in next double crochet, chain 1) around. Join in top of chain 3.

Round 30: Chain 4. (double crochet in next double crochet, chain 1) 6 times. Double crochet next two double crochets together, chain 1; (double crochet in next double crochet, chain 1) 6 times; double crochet the next 2 double crochets together, chain 1; (double crochet in next double crochet, chain 1) 6 times, double crochet the next 2 double crochets together, chain 1, double crochet in next double crochet, chain 1) 6 times; double crochet the next 2 double crochets together, chain 1; double crochet in next double crochet, chain 1) 6 times; double crochet the next 2 double crochets together, chain 1; double crochet in next double crochet, chain 1) 6 times; double crochet the next 2 double crochets together, chain 1; double crochet in next double crochet, chain 1) 6 times; double crochet the next 2 double crochets together, chain 1;(double crochet in next double crochet, chain 1) until the end; join in top of chain 3.

Round 31: Chain 3. Work (1 double crochet in chain 1 space, 1 double crochet in next double crochet) around. Join in top of chain 3 space.

Round 32: Chain 3. Double crochet in each double crochet around.

Round 33: Chain 2. Half double crochet in next 8 stitches. Place a marker in the stitch just made.

Half double crochet next 4 stitches, half double crochet next two stitches together. Half double crochet next 12 stitches, half double crochet the next two stitches together. Half double crochet in next 4 stitches, place marker in stitch just made. Half double crochet in next 8 stitches, half double crochet next two stitches together. Half double crochet in next 6 stitches, place marker in the stitch just made, half double crochet in next 6 stitches, half double crochet next two stitches together, half double crochet in next 12 stitches, half double crochet next two stitches together, half double crochet in next 2 stitches, place marker in the stitch just made, half double crochet until the end. Join in top of chain 2.

Fasten off and weave in the ends.

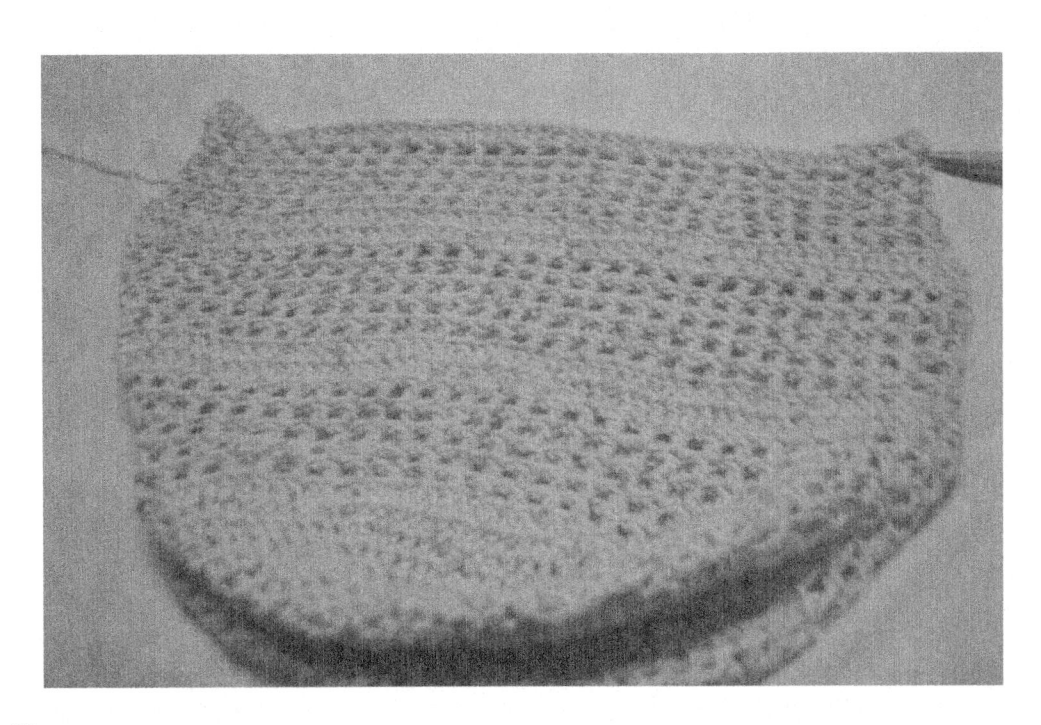

Handle

Note: Until specified, the following rows are worked without turning chains.

Row 1: With right side facing, attach the yarn with a slip stitch to the stitch before the marker.

Remove the marker, and half double crochet each stitch to the next marker. Remove that marker. Slip stitch in the next stitch, turn.

Row 2: Half double crochet the next 2 stitches together.

Half double crochet to last 2 stitches, half double crochet the last two stitches together. Turn work.

Row 3: Half double crochet the next 2 stitches together, half double crochet the next 2 stitches together, half double crochet to the last 2 stitches, half double crochet the last 2 stitches together. Turn work.

Repeat row three until only 5 stitches remain.

Chain 2. Half double crochet until the end. Turn. Repeat this row 15 times, fasten off, leaving a tail.

Repeat the process for the other side.

Now you have two unfinished edges. Hold the wrong sides together and use a single crochet stitch to fasten them together.

Optional

Attach yarn to any stitch of the top edge of the bag, with right side facing you, and single crochet around. Fasten off and do the same on the other side to give a finished appearance to the bag.

Granny Square Rug

This classic design has taken on a modern twist! The granny square is one of the oldest and most popular crocheted motifs, and here is a pattern showcasing the timeless design in a modern way. This rug will warm cold feet and make your heart happy!

Supplies Needed

H/8 (1.5 mm) crochet hook

Multiple colors of yarn. (I used Red Heart Super Saver, 1 skein each of Dusty Gray (color A) // Sea Coral (color B) // True Blue (color C))

Pattern Notes

Change colors at every round in a random pattern. Leave a 3" long tail and crochet over the top of it when working the next row to have less work weaving in the ends at the end. Do not turn work — everything is worked in the round.

You need 6 total squares of the pattern below. The colors I used are as follows:

Square 1: A // C // B // A // C // B

Square 2: B // A // C // A // B // C

Square 3: C // B // A // C // B // C

Square 4: B // B // C // A // B // A

Square 5: C // A // B // C // B // A

Square 6: B // C // A // B // B // A

Because I chose to use variegated yarn skeins, I pulled from both ends to give me different shades and colors as I worked. Go ahead and mix and match your yarns and make it yours — the mixing up and randomness of this project is what makes it so unique!

Pattern

Round 1: Chain 6. Join with a slip stitch to the last chain.

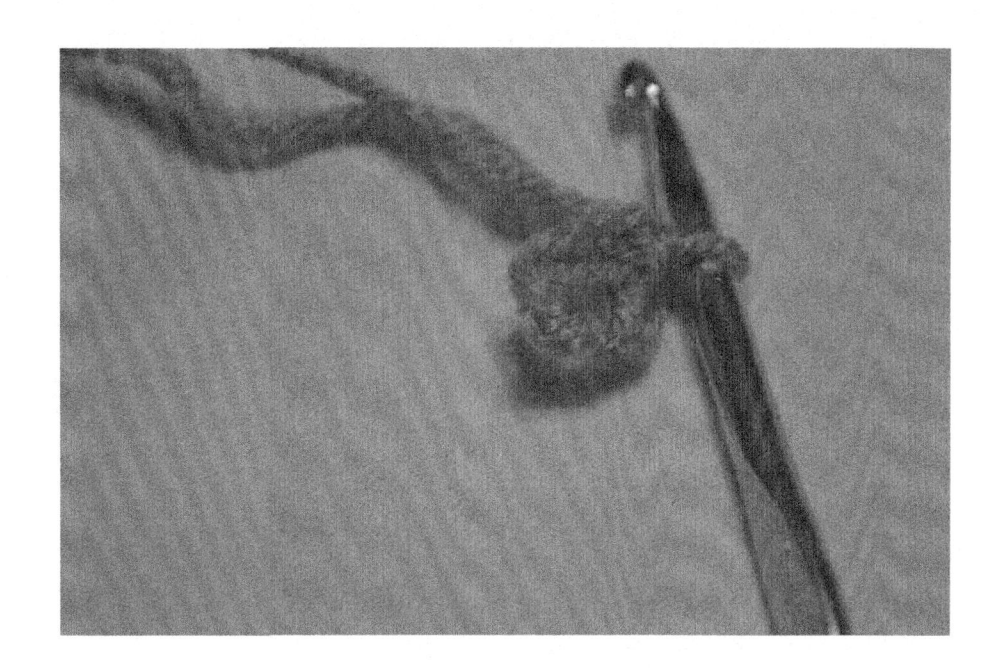

Chain 3 (counts as the first double crochet here and throughout).

2 double crochet in the loop.

Chain 2, 3 double crochet in the loop.

Chain 2, 3 double crochet in the loop, chain 2, 3 double crochet in the loop, chain 2. Join with slip stitch to top of first chain 3, Fasten off.

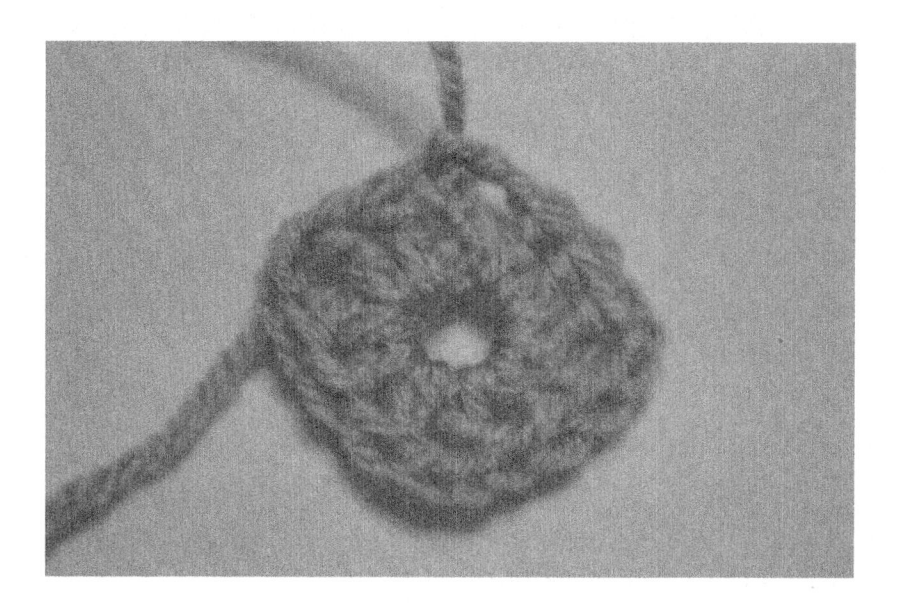

Round 2: Attach new color with a slip stitch to any of the corner chains.

Chain 3.

2 double crochet in the same space.

Chain 2, work 3 double crochet in the *same* space.

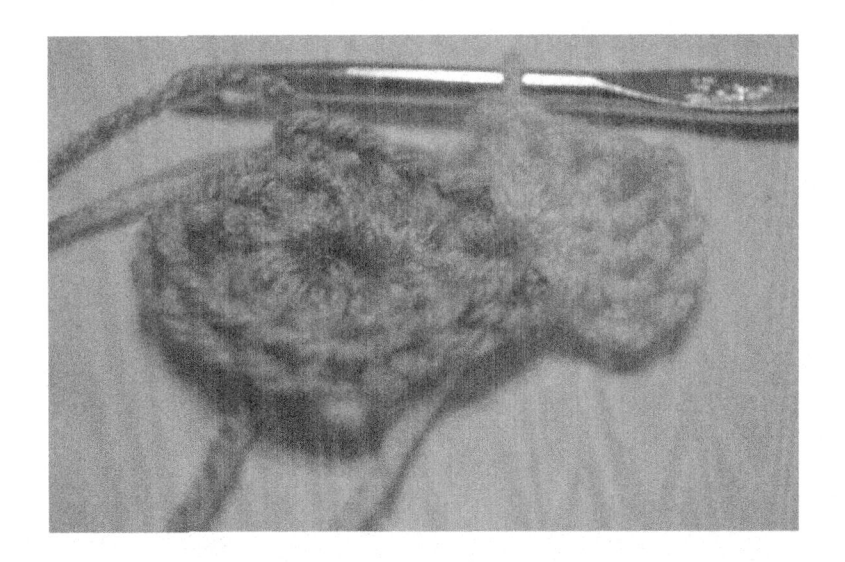

(3 double crochet, chain 2, 3 double crochet) in each corner around. Join with slip stitch in the top of first chain 3. Fasten off.

Round 3: Attach new color with a slip stitch to any of the corner chains. 2 double crochet in the same space, chain 2, 3 double crochet in the same space.

3 double crochet in the next space.

(3 double crochet, chain 2, 3 double crochet) in the next chain 2 space, 3 double crochet in next space. Continue in this manner until the end. Join with slip stitch to beginning chain 3. Fasten off.

Round 4: Attach new color with a slip stitch to any of the corner chains. Chain 3, 2 double crochet in the same space, chain 2, 3 double crochet in the same space. (3 double crochet in next space) until you reach the corner; 3 double crochet, chain 2, 3 double crochet in the corner chain 2 space; (3 double crochet in next space) until the corner; 3 double crochet, chain 2, 3 double crochet in the corner chain 2 space, (3 double crochet in next space) until you reach the corner, 3 double crochet, chain 2, 3 double crochet in the corner chain 2 space; (3 double crochet in next space) until you reach the end; join with slip stitch to the top of first chain 3. Fasten off.

Round 5: Attach new color with a slip stitch to any of the corner chains. Chain 3, 2 double crochet in the same space, chain 2, 3 double crochet in the same space. (3 double crochet in next space) until you reach the corner; 3 double crochet, chain 2, 3 double crochet in the corner chain 2 space; (3 double crochet in next space) until the corner; 3 double crochet, chain 2, 3 double crochet in the corner chain 2 space, (3 double crochet in next space) until you reach the corner, 3 double crochet, chain 2, 3 double crochet in the corner chain 2 space; (3 double crochet in next space) until you reach the end; join with slip stitch to the top of first chain 3. Fasten off.

Round 6: Attach new color with a slip stitch to any of the corner chains. Chain 3, 2 double crochet in the same space, chain 2, 3 double crochet in the same space. (3 double crochet in next space) until you reach the corner; 3 double crochet, chain 2, 3 double crochet in the corner chain 2 space; (3 double crochet in next space) until the corner; 3 double crochet, chain 2, 3 double crochet in the corner chain 2 space, (3 double crochet in next space) until you reach the corner, 3 double crochet, chain 2, 3 double crochet in the corner chain 2 space; (3 double crochet in next space) until you reach the end; join with slip stitch to the top of first chain 3. Fasten off.

Repeat this process until you have 6 squares.

Lay the squares out on a flat surface until you are satisfied with the design.

Using any color yarn (I used B) single crochet the short ends of all the squares together.

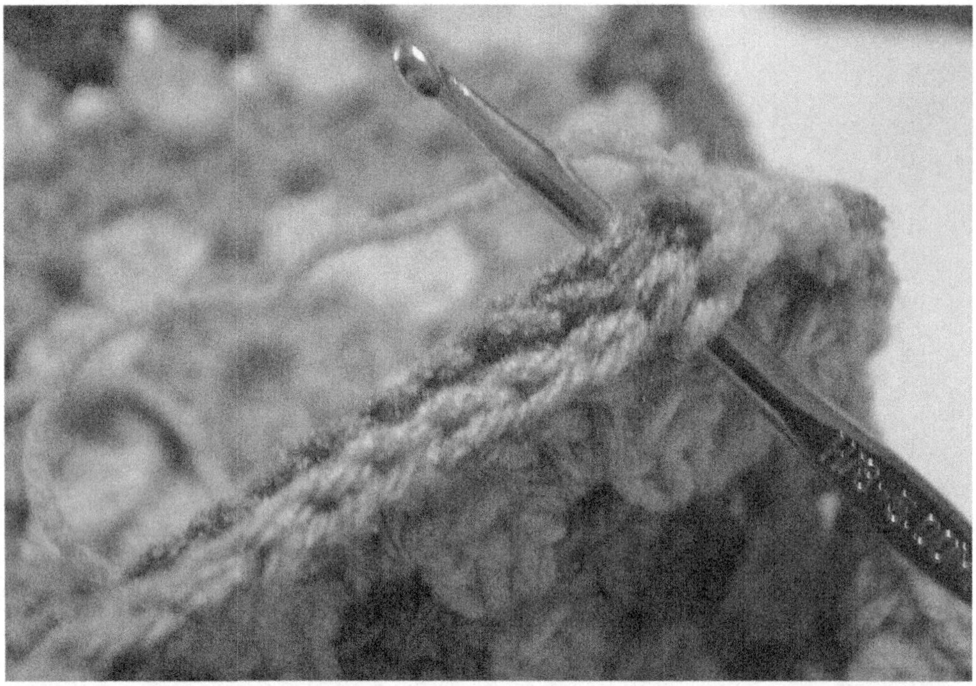

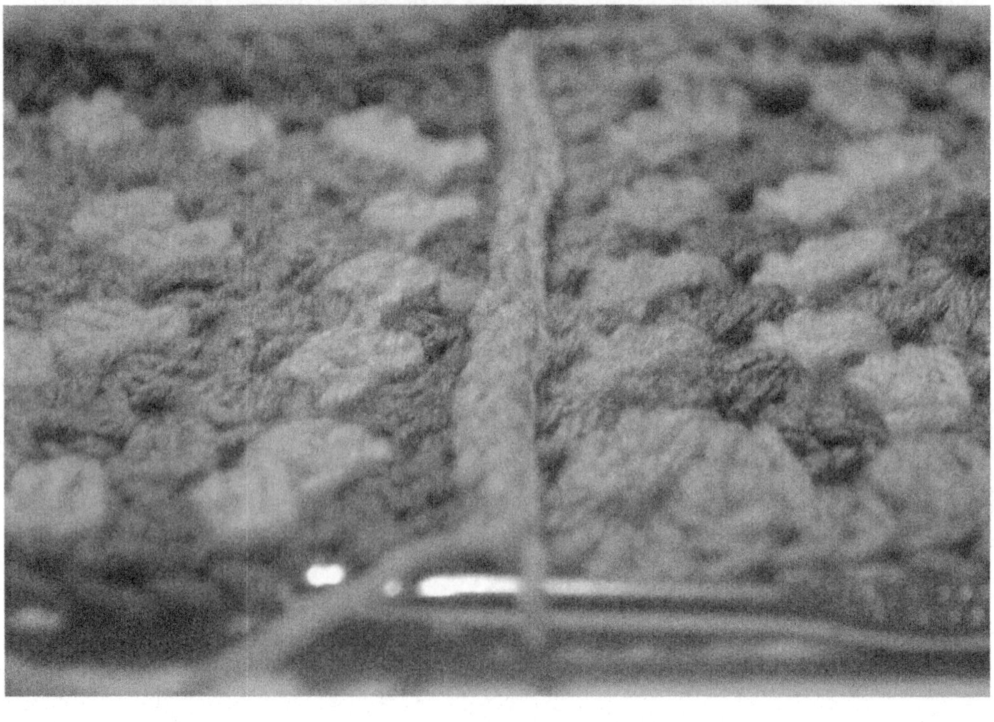

Now hold both long pieces you created together and using the same color (B), single crochet them both together all the way down.

Using the same color (B), single crochet in each double crochet all the way around the large rectangle you have created, with the right side facing you, placing 3 single crochet stitches into each chain 2 corner.

Place a stitch marker in the middle of the group of three single crochets. Join with slip stitch to beginning stitch, fasten off.

Take your yarn and cut lengths of it. They should measure somewhere between 1 foot and 3 feet long — they shouldn't all be the same length, and they should be random.

Using these pieces, randomly join yarn at any point of the rug, right side facing.

Chain 1. Single crochet around, placing three single crochet stitches into the marked stitch of the corner and moving the marker up as you go. As you run out of yarn, join a new piece.

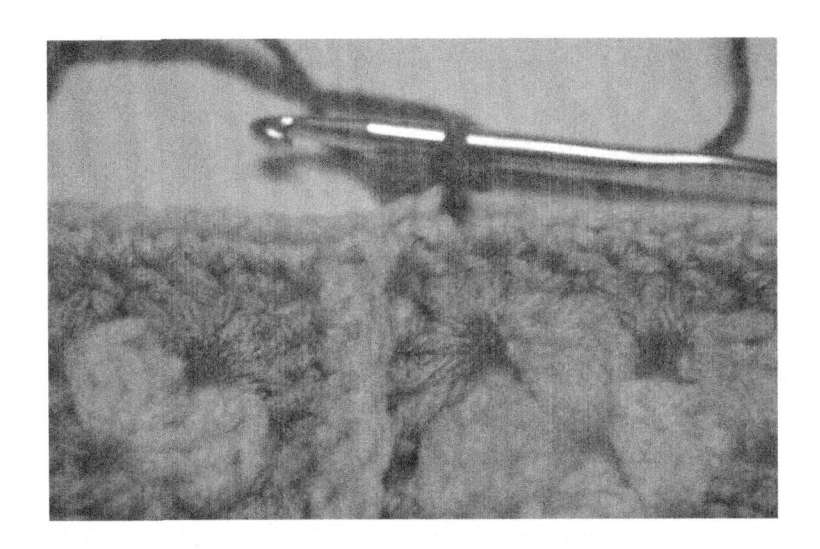

Slip stitch at end to beginning chain, fasten off, and start in a different place for the next round.

Repeat this process until the border measures 3 inches. Fasten off and weave in ends.

Soap Sack

Tired of washcloths and bars of soap slipping away from you? That is a thing of the past with this handy little sack! This absorbent bag made of cotton yarn is the perfect way to contain that bar of soap. It's like a washcloth — only the soap is inside! Just lather up and wash!

Supplies Needed

Approximately 2 oz. 100% cotton yarn. (I used 1 skein Peaches and Creme cotton; 2.5oz.)

G/6 - 4.25 mm crochet hook

Pattern

Row 1: Leaving a long tail, chain 21.

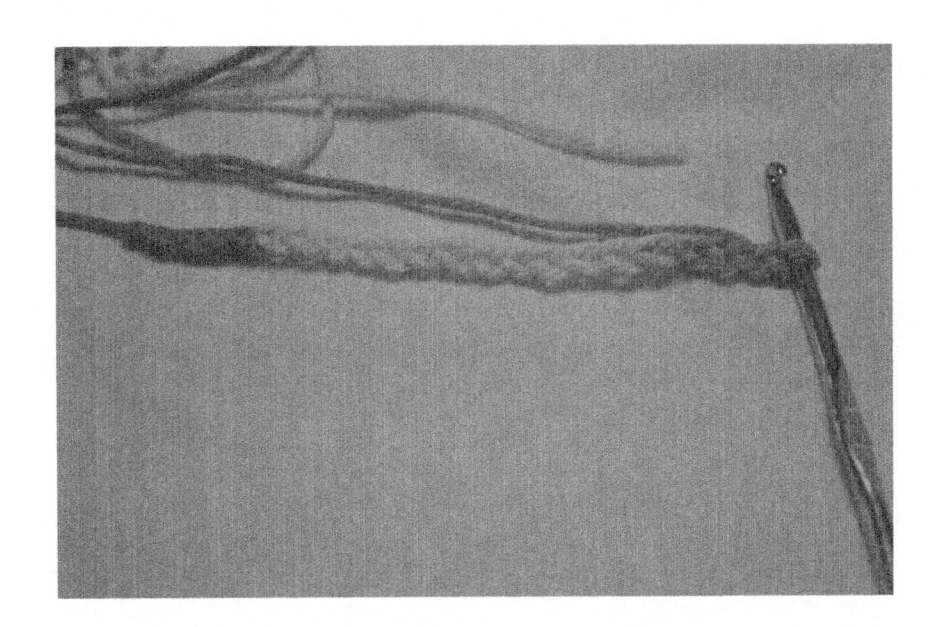

Double crochet in 3rd chain from hook.

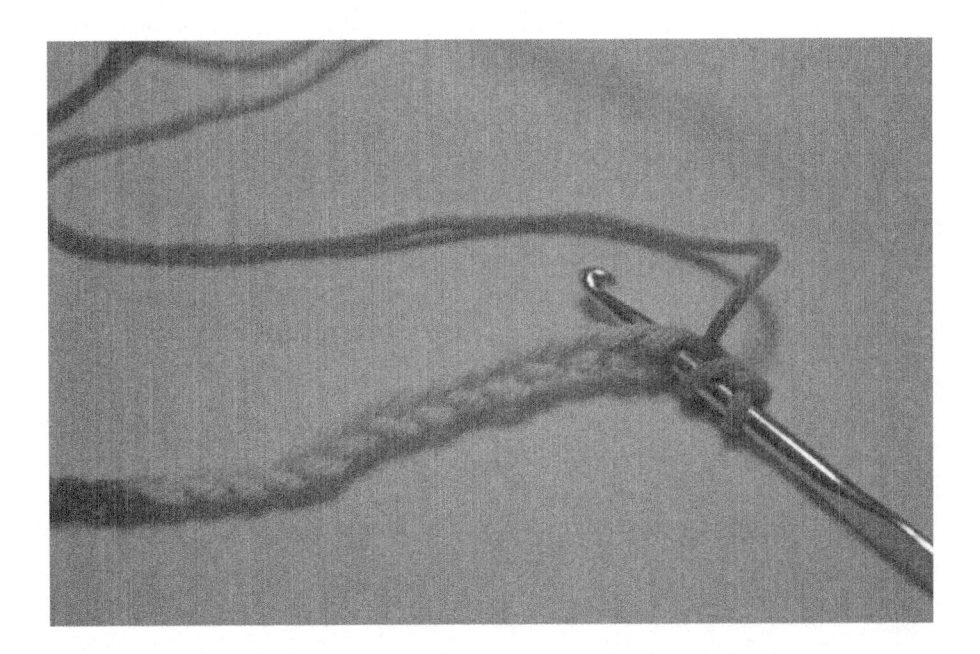

Double crochet in each chain across. Turn. *18 double crochet stitches.*

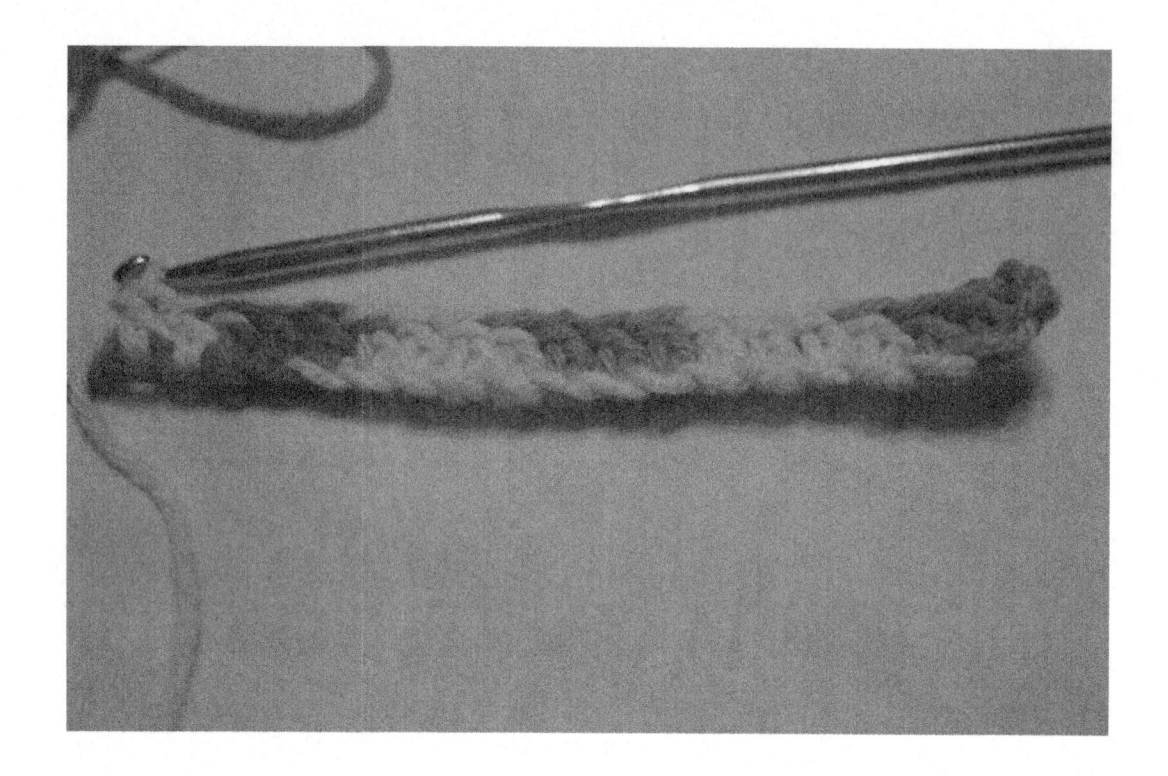

Row 2: Chain 4.

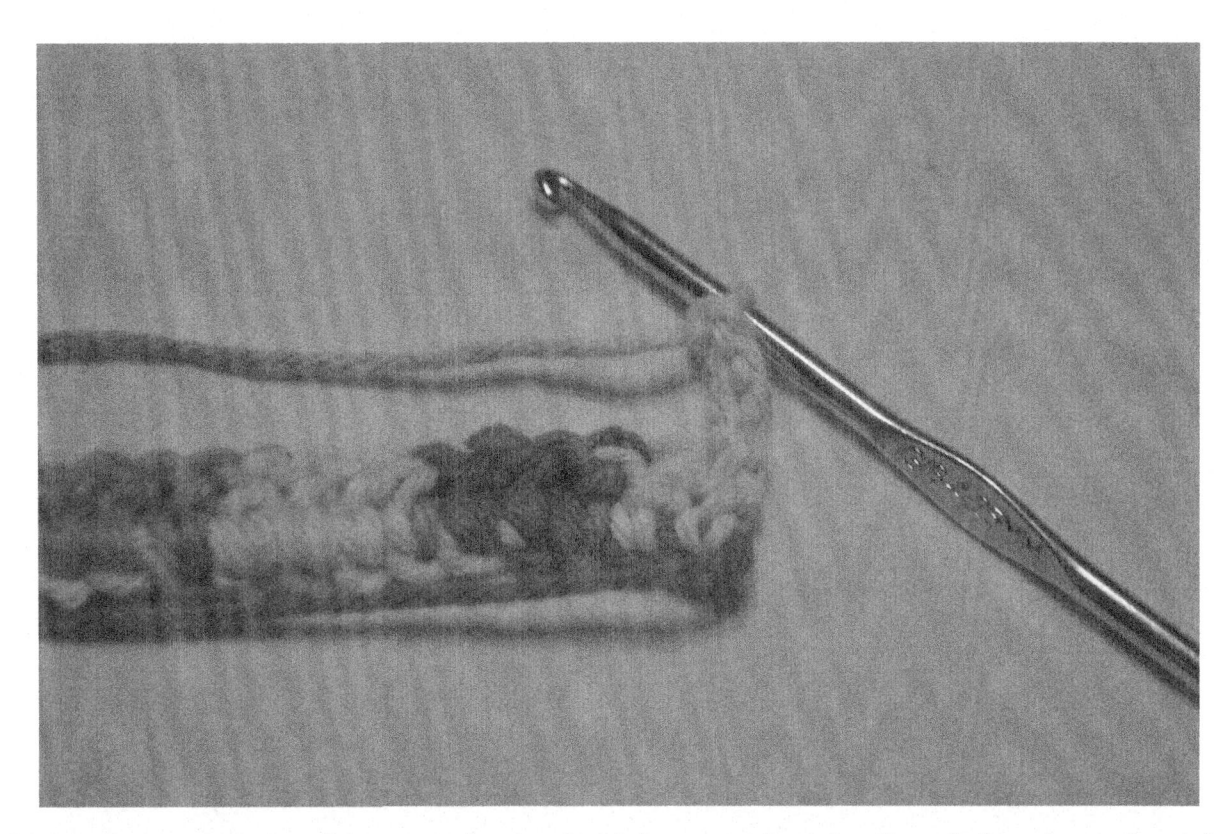

Skip the next double crochet, double crochet in the following double crochet.

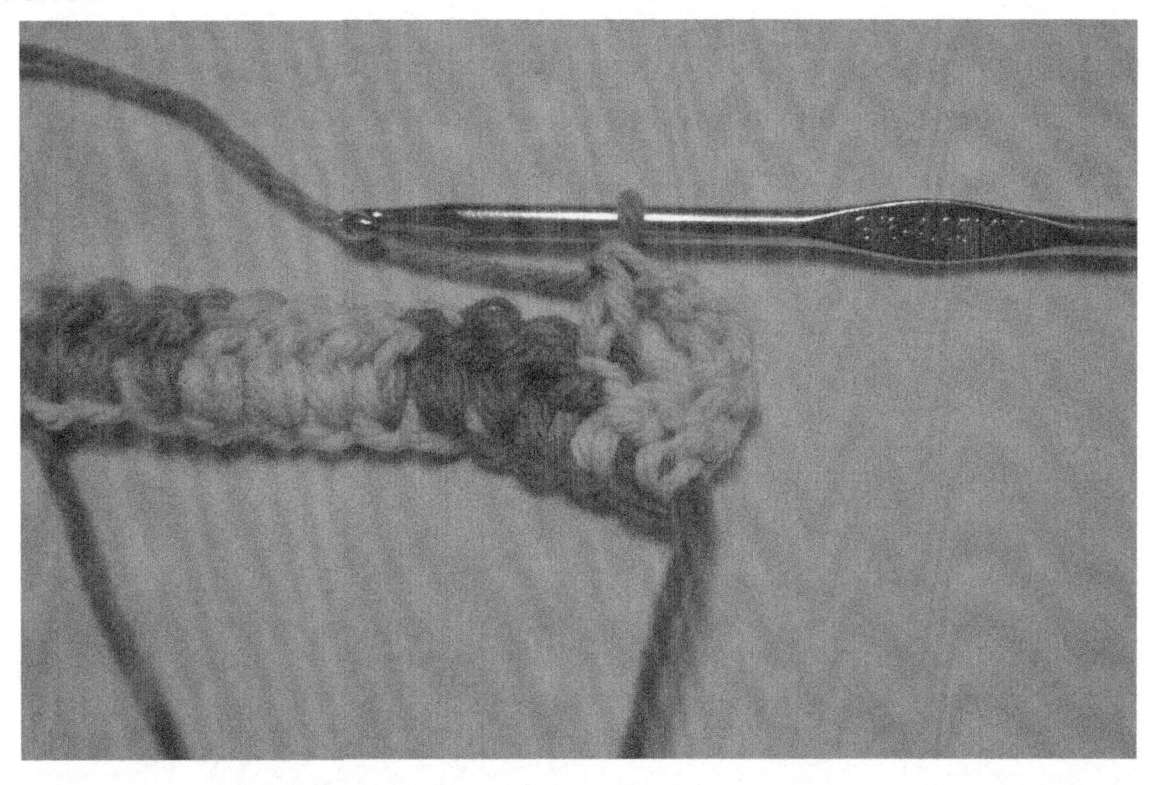

*Chain 1, skip the next double crochet, double crochet in the following double crochet. Repeat from (*) across. Turn.

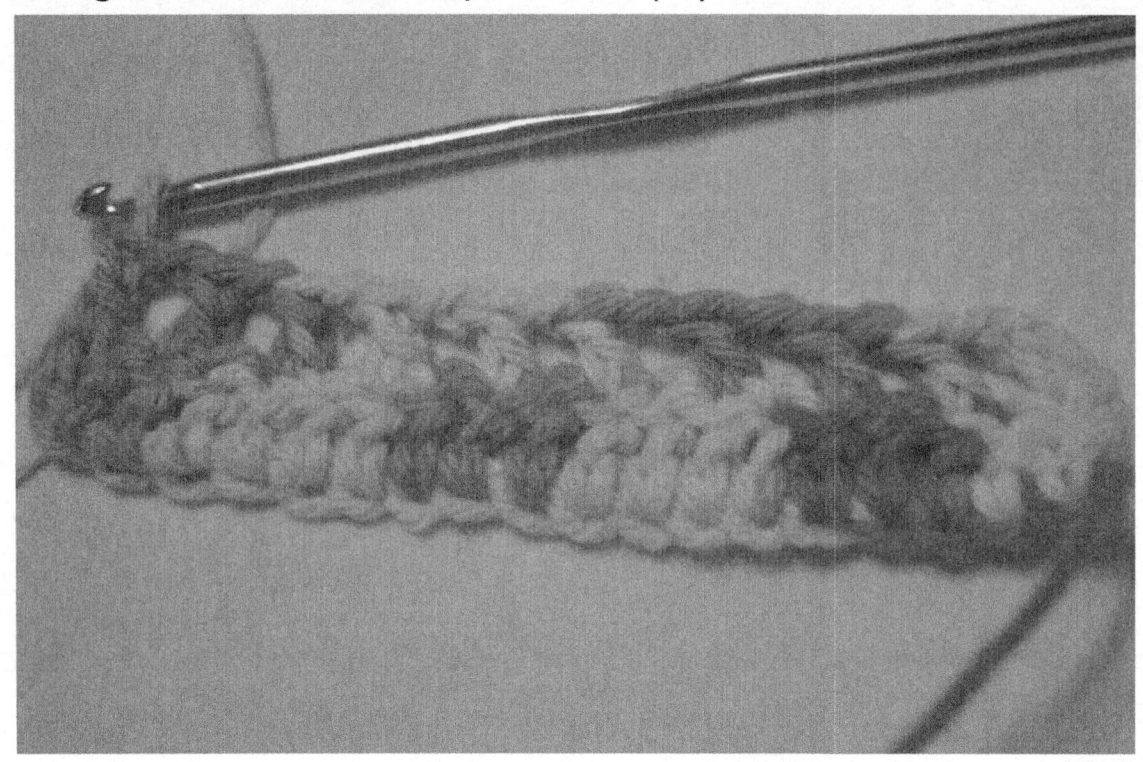

Row 3: Chain 2. Counts as the first half double crochet here and throughout the pattern. *Slip stitch in the chain 1 space.

Half double crochet in the double crochet stitch.

Repeat from * across. Turn.

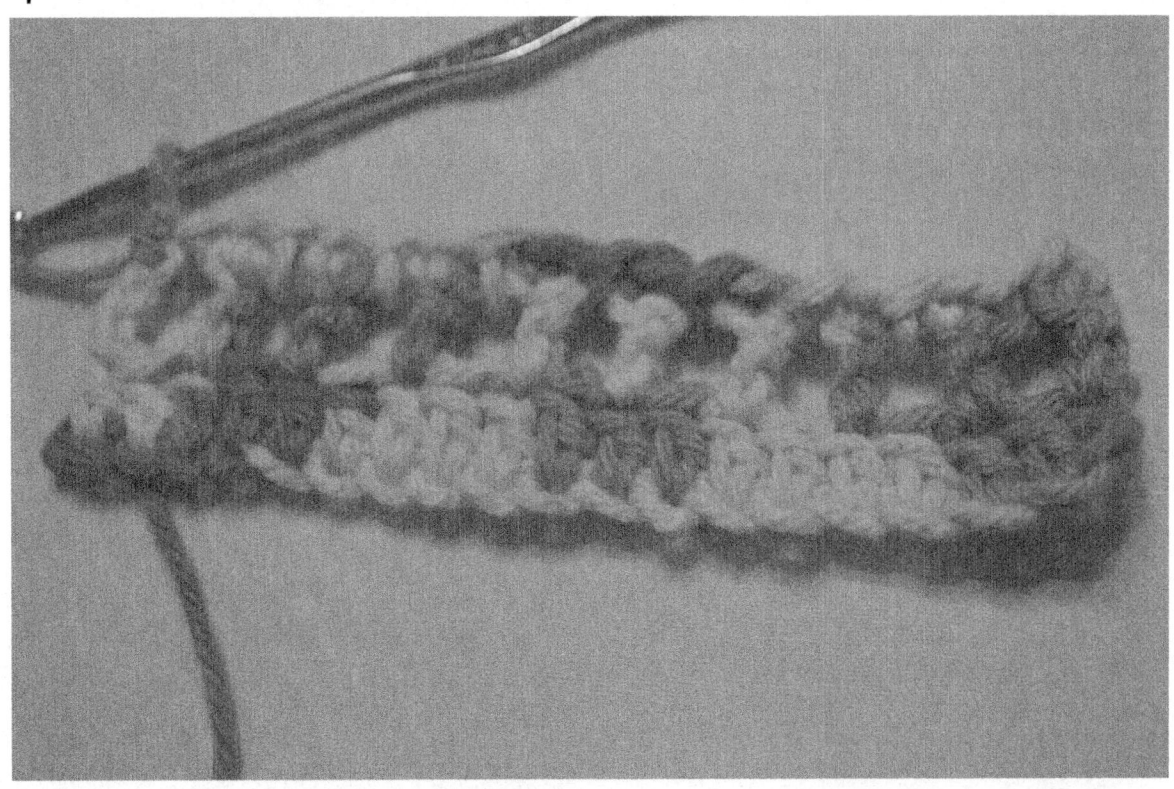

Row 4: Chain 1. Counts as the first slip stitch here and throughout the pattern.

*Half double crochet in next slip stitch; slip stitch in next half double crochet. Repeat from (*) across. Turn.

Row 5: Chain 2. *Slip stitch in next half double crochet stitch, half double crochet in next slip stitch. Repeat from (*) across. Turn.

Row 6 - Row 46: Repeat rows 4 and 5 for 20 more times.

Row 47: Chain 4. *Skip slip stitch, double crochet in half double crochet, chain 1. Repeat from (*) across. Turn.

Row 48: Chain 3. *Double crochet in next chain 1 space, double crochet in next double crochet. Repeat from (*) across. Fasten off.

Finishing

Fold piece in half.

Using a crochet hook or a darning needle, sew up the long edges.

Weave in the ends and turn right side out.

Chain 120. Fasten off and weave in ends.

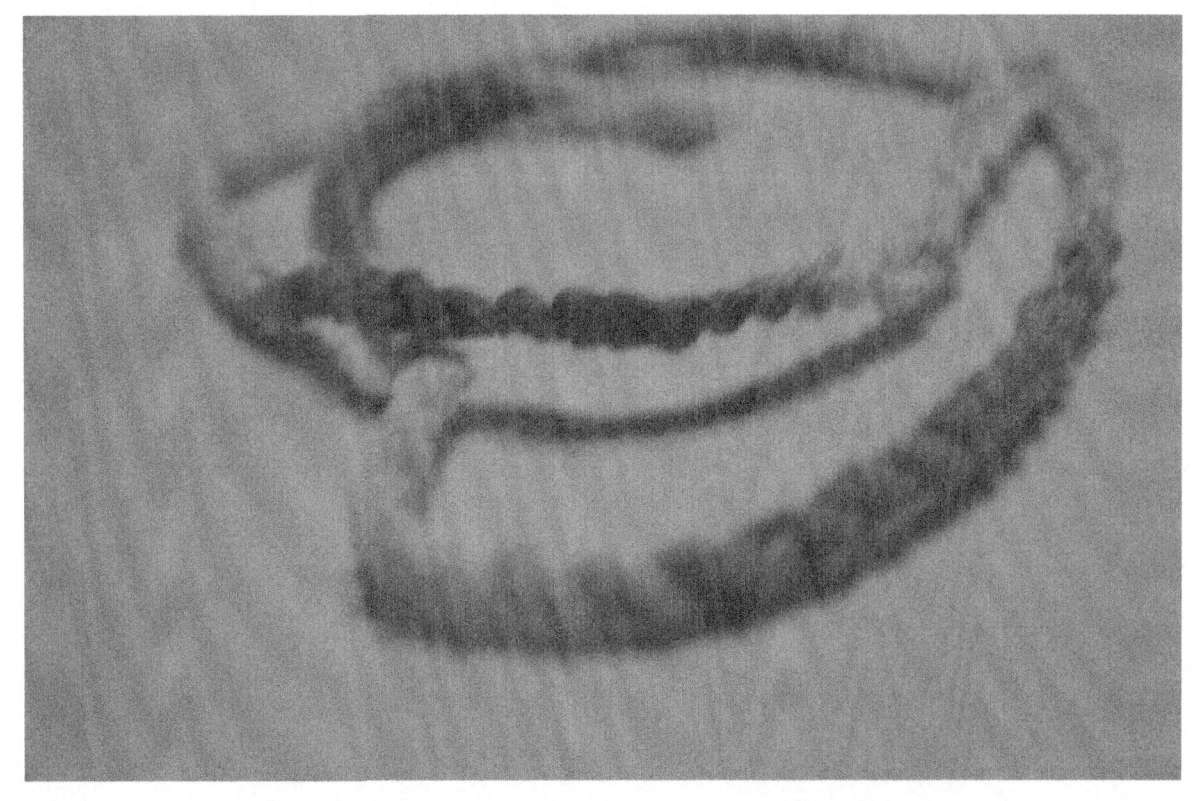

Weave chain through the double crochet, chain 1 round.

Add soap, pull tight, and tie.

Cozy Cowl

This cowl pattern uses an intricate stitch pattern to create an elegant and unique accessory to your winter wardrobe! Warm and comfy, you won't be able to stop at just one. Soon every single friend you have will be able to boast of owning a handmade creation straight from your hook!

This pattern is ideal for variegated yarns, as the pattern helps to break up the variegation, and you can see the individual colors. It is also an elegant piece to work up in one color - whatever you choose to do, have fun with it!

Supplies Needed

1 skein (3.5 oz. // 262 yds) size 3 yarn — I used Yarn Bee Must be Merino; color way mint/gray

J/6.0mm crochet hook

2 1 1/4" diameter decorative buttons

Pattern

Chain 57.

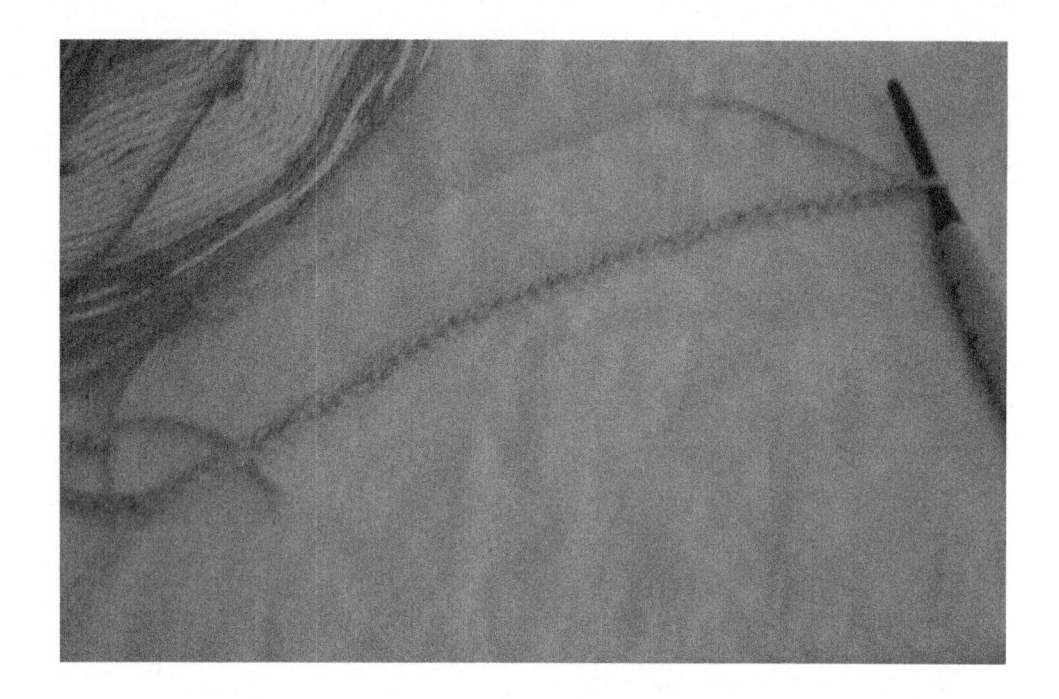

Row 1: 2 Double crochet in 4th chain from hook.

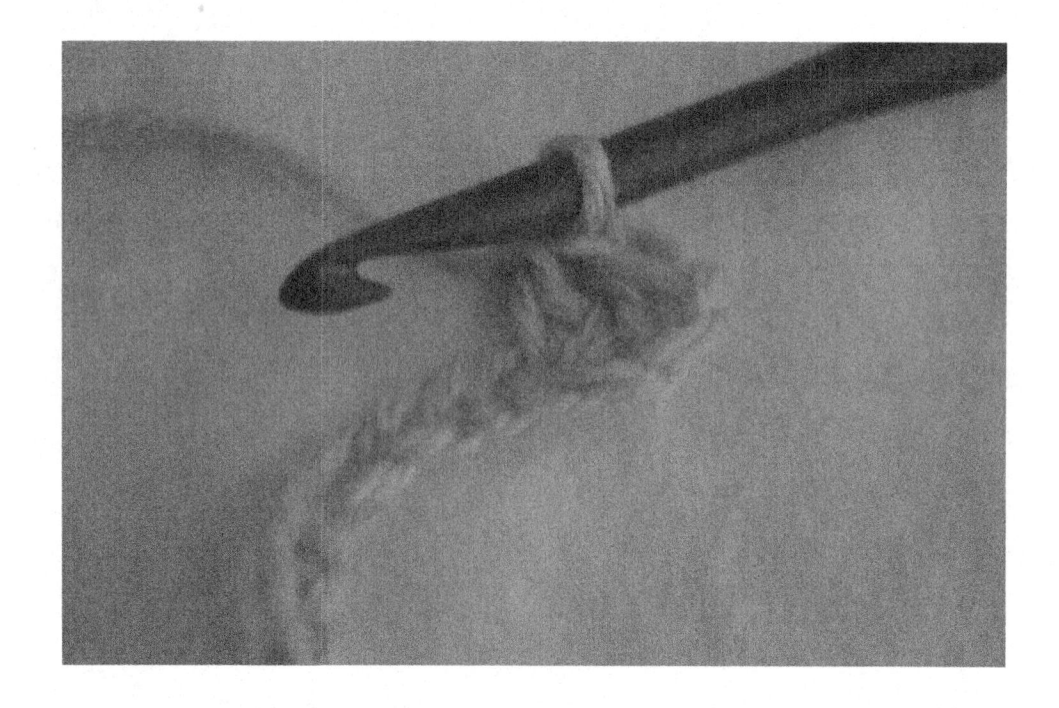

*Skip 3 chains. Single crochet in the next chain.

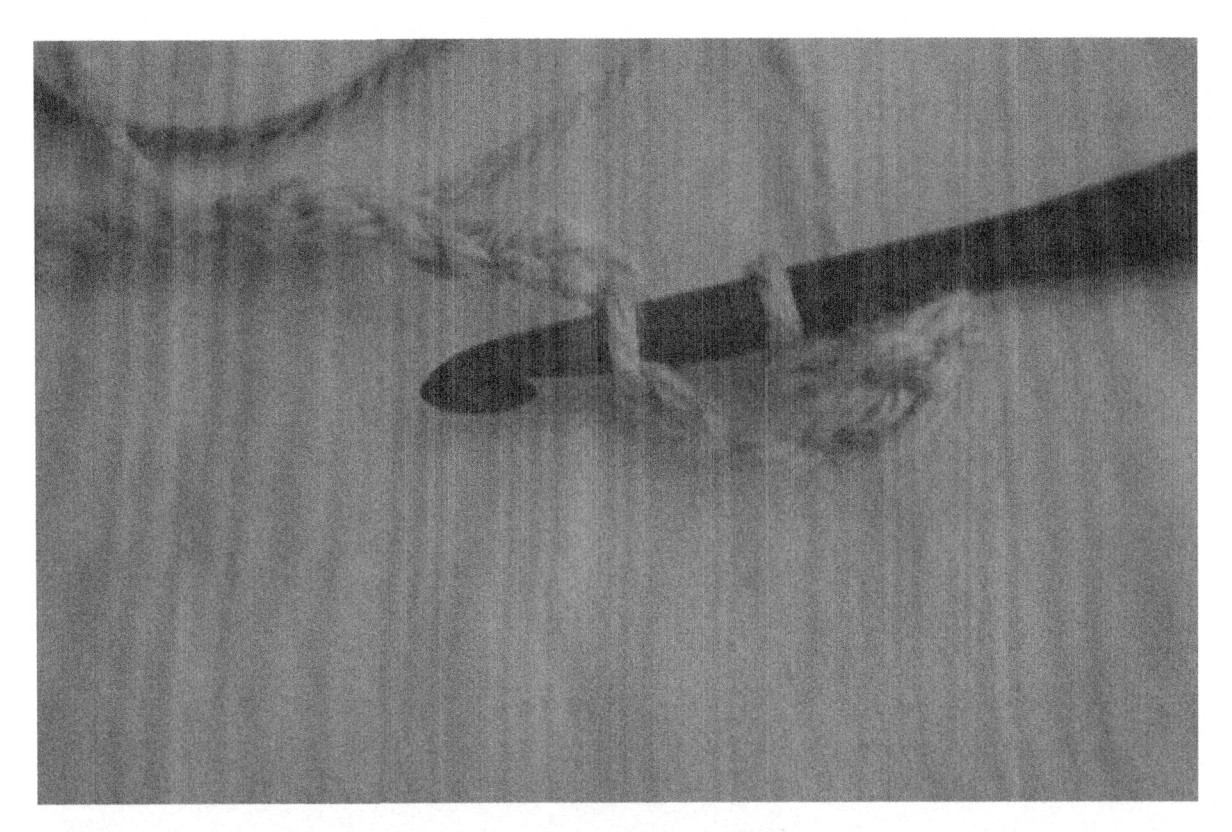

Chain 2. Double crochet in the next 3 chains.

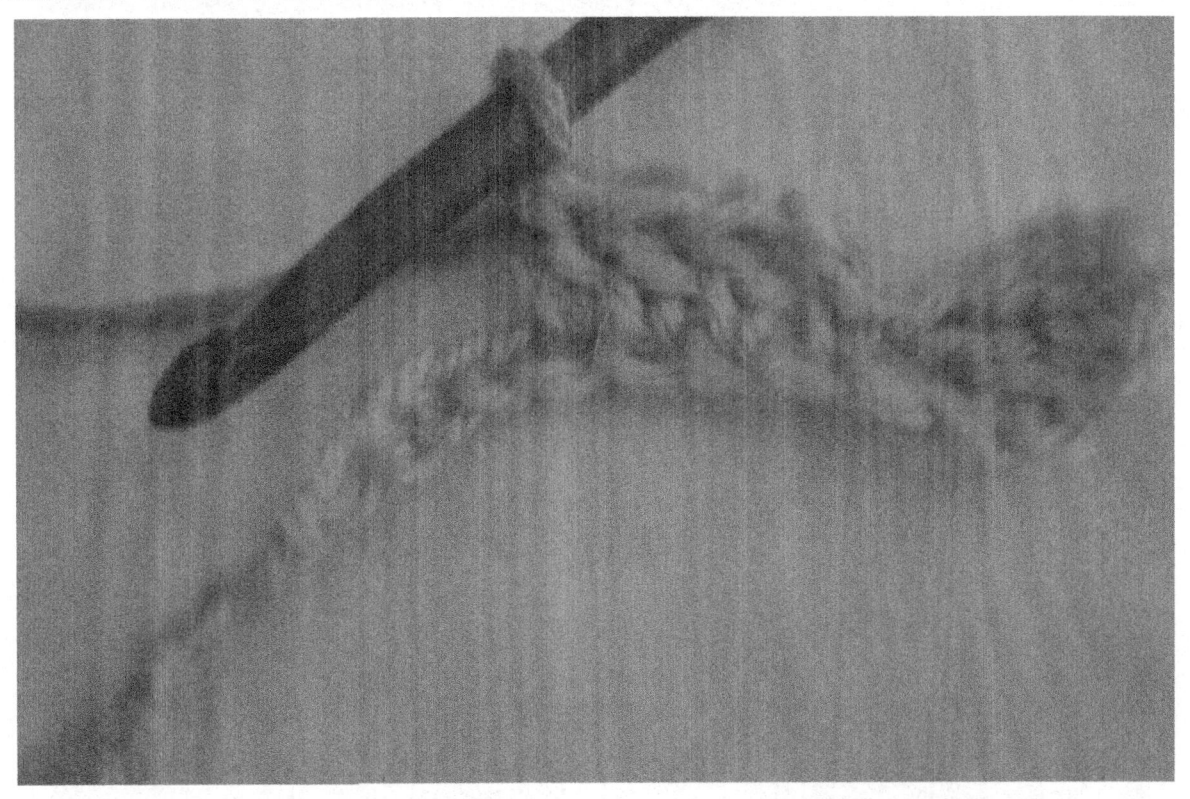

Repeat from the (*) across the remaining chains. End with a single crochet in the last chain.

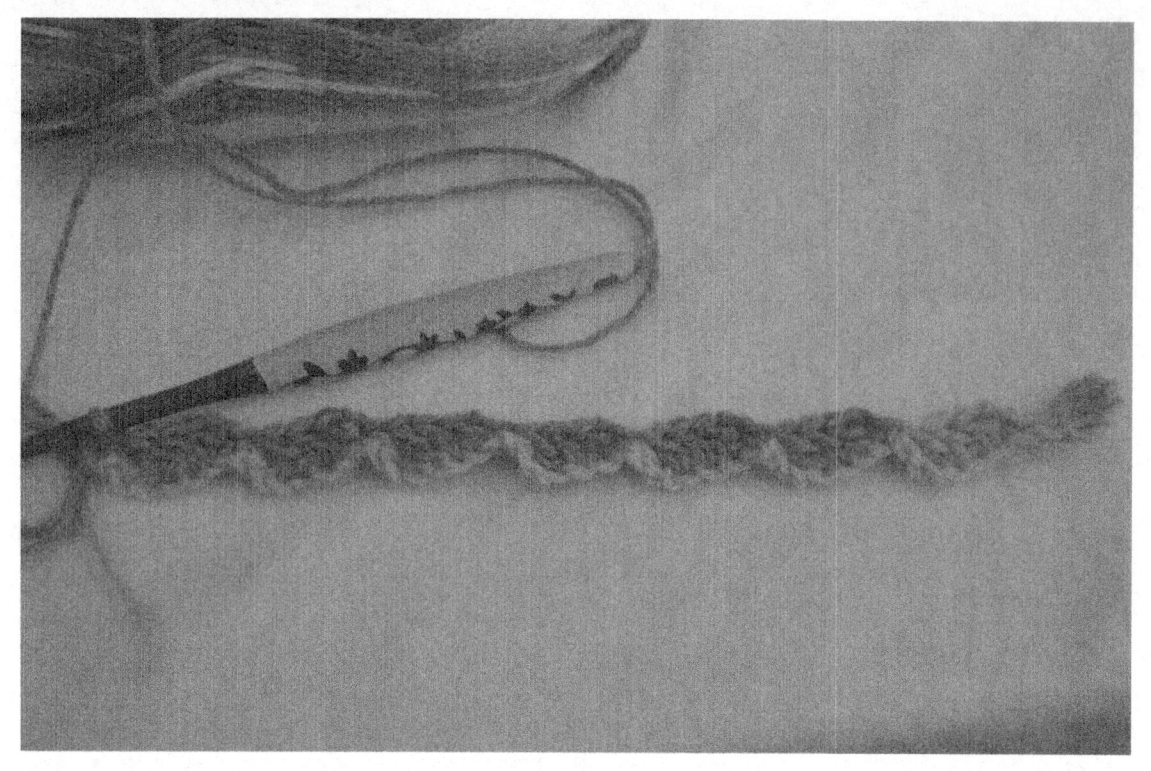

Turn.

Row 2: Chain 3.

2 Double crochet in first single crochet.

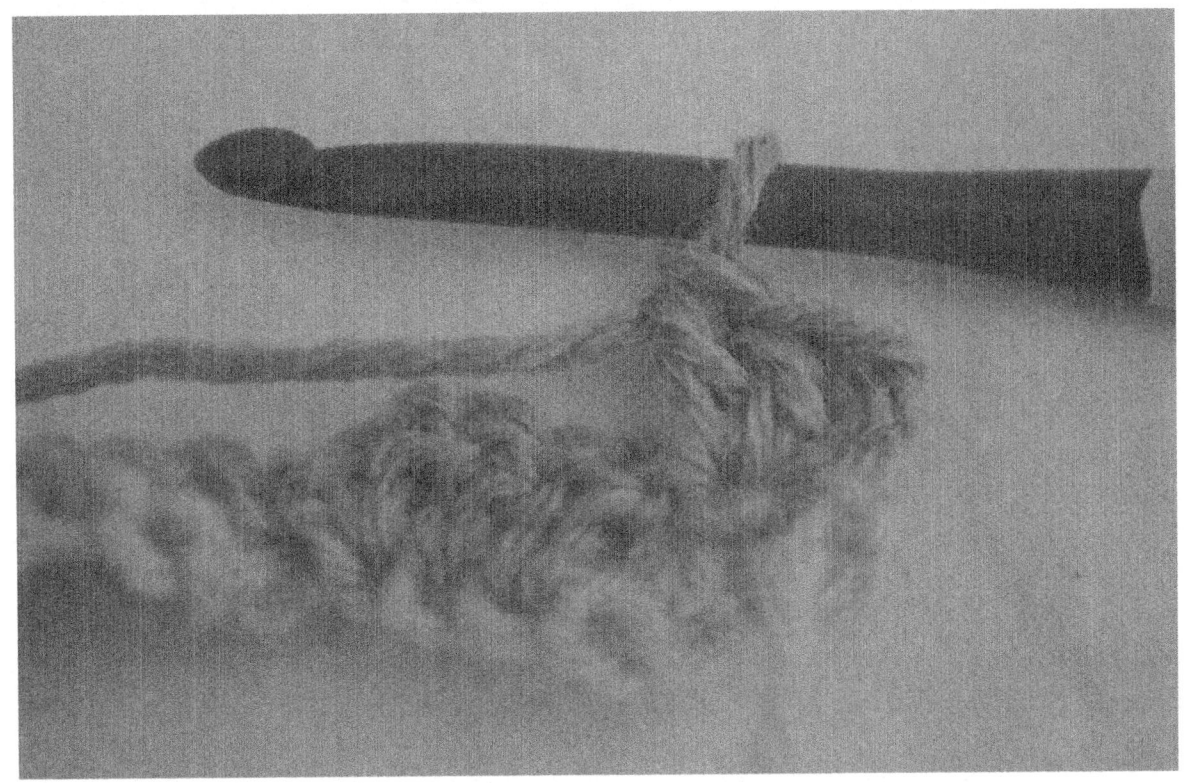

*Skip to the next chain 2 space from the previous row, and single crochet in the top of it.

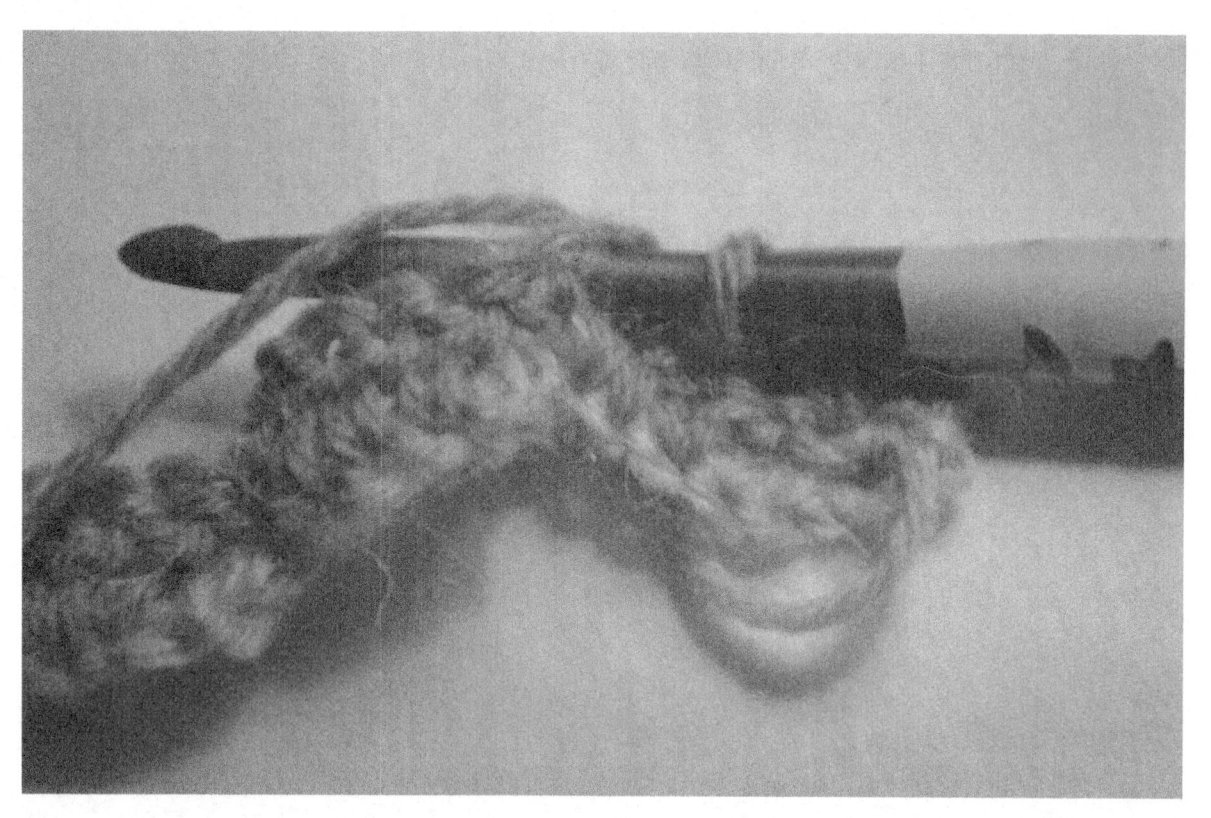

Chain 2.

3 double crochet into the same space.

Repeat from (*) to the end of the row, ending with a single crochet in the top of the turning chain of the previous round. Turn work.

You should begin to see a pattern of tiny squares emerging!

Repeat row 2 again…

And again …

And again …

Until the piece measures 26".

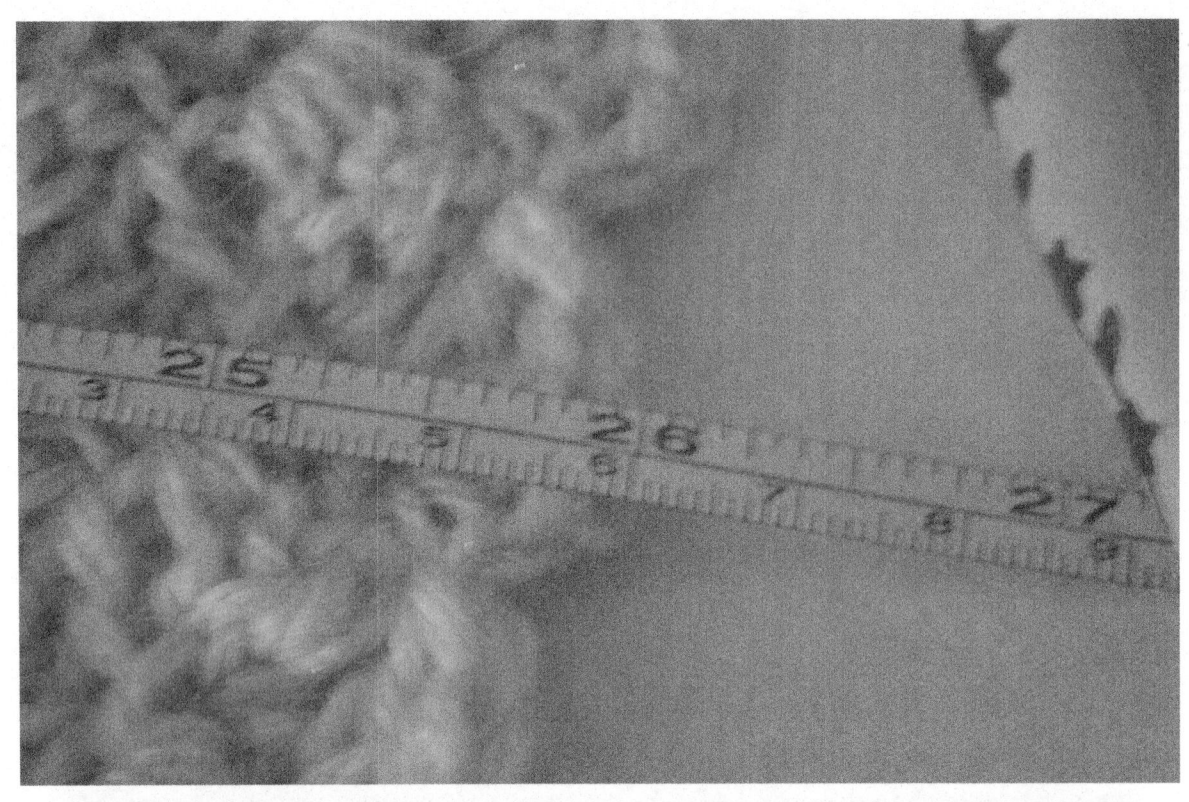

Buttonhole Row:

Row 1: Chain 3. 2 double crochet in the first single crochet, skip to the next chain 2 space. Single crochet in the top of the chain 2 space, chain 2, and 3 double crochet in the same space. Single crochet in top of next chain 2 space, chain 5.

Single crochet in the top of the next chain 2 space.

Chain 5.

*Single crochet in top of next chain 2 space.

Chain 2. 3 double crochet in the same space. Repeat from the (*) to the end, ending with a single crochet in the top of the turning chain from the previous row. Turn.

Row 2: Chain 3. 2 double crochet in the first single crochet, skip to the next chain 2 space. *Single crochet in the top of the next chain 2 space, chain 2, 3 double crochet in the same space. Repeat from (*) four times. Single crochet in the 3rd chain of the chain 5 from the previous row.

Chain 2.

3 double crochet in the chain 5 space. Make sure you go into the space and not through the chain!

Single crochet in the 3rd chain of the next chain 5 space.

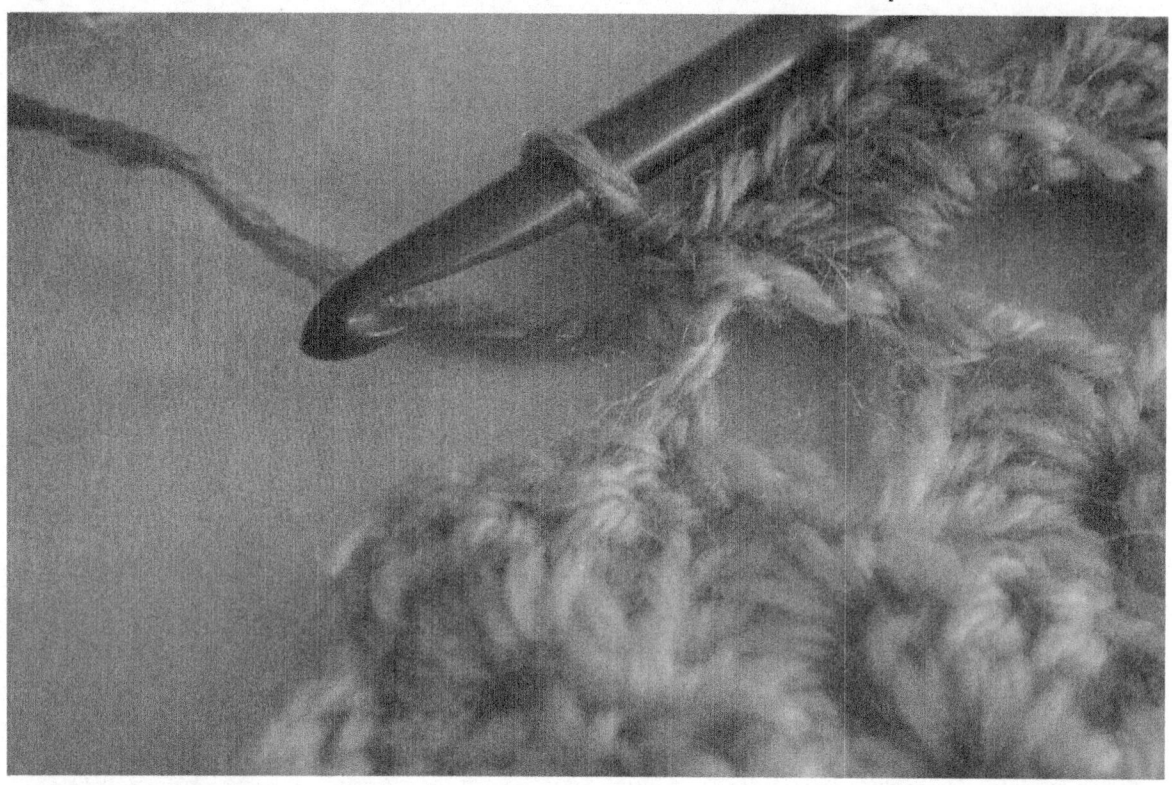

Chain 2

3 double crochet in the space — again, make sure you go into the space and not through the chain!

Single crochet in next chain 2 space, chain 2, 3 double crochet in the same space. Single crochet in the top of the turning chain, and fasten off. Cut yarn and weave in ends.

Finishing:

Fold the piece so that the ends overlap, with the buttonholes on top. Mark where the buttons need to go. Using a yarn needle and a piece of yarn, sew the buttons on.

148

Conclusion

Just pour me my coffee, hand me my crochet, and slowly back away.

Crocheting is a fun and worthwhile pastime that is well worth learning! It is addictive, as you've probably discovered by now. As you grow in your skills, you'll find that there is an endless supply of new projects to try and new yarns to buy. You'll notice that you can spend hours looking up and down the yarn aisle; your friends will think that they've lost you only to discover you're still looking at yarn.

The adage that says, "If at first you don't succeed, try, try again!" certainly applies to crochet. It may take a while to get the perfect stitches so you can make the perfect item, but don't give up! Instead of focusing on perfection, focus on the fun there is in creation, the skills you're learning, and permit yourself to have at it.

Remember, these patterns are just a beginning, and many of them can be customized to meet your unique preferences. The colors and fibers can be mixed and matched to reflect your personality. You should also feel free to pick up a hook and yarn without a pattern and see what you can create. The options indeed are endless!

Happy Hooking!

Troubleshooting

A loop after a loop. Hour after hour my madness becomes crochet.
Life and art are inseparable. — Olek

Problem: I can't get my crochet hook through the stitch!

Take a deep breath and calm down! You are crocheting too tightly — try to loosen up the yarn between your fingers. Let it go, lay it on the table, get something to drink, and when you come back, the problem should be solved! Also, try slipping the loop of yarn farther up the hook to loosen it up.

Problem: There's no stitch definition! It all looks like one big, tangled up mess!

Your stitches are way too loose, my friend! Hold the yarn tighter as you work each stitch, and make sure to pull each stitch snug against the handle of the crochet hook.

Problem: My project is sloping inward on the sides, towards the middle.

Count your stitches. Now read through your pattern and see if it gives you a stitch count. If it doesn't, no worries! Look over your project and make sure that you are catching the last "stitch" — you know, the one made by the turning chain.

If you are catching that stitch, and the project is really sloping, check your tension and make sure your rows aren't being crocheted tighter than they were before.

If all of that is good, look back over your project and see if you find one spot thicker than the fabric around it — it's possible that you've accidentally crocheted two stitches together, and will need to go back and fix it.

Problem: Each row I work is growing longer!!

Woah! Don't panic — just count your stitches and see if they match up with the pattern count. If there's no count, look really close at the sides of your work. It's possible that in an effort to make sure you catch every single last stitch, you are placing two stitches into the turning chain at the end. It's also possible that you are placing a stitch into the beginning stitch of the row, and are forgetting about your turning chain.

If that's not the culprit, look carefully at your work and see if there's a place where you are crocheting two stitches into one.

If that doesn't solve it, check your tension. Your yarn may have grown looser in your hand. Just go back and tighten it up!

Printed in Great Britain
by Amazon